Greek Cuisine

An easy guide for everyone

Photography & Copyright: Douwe Hoogstins
Translation: Diane Shugart
Cover: Kostas Houhoulis

ISBN 960-406-050-3

Mirsini Lampraki

Greek Cuisine

An easy guide for everyone

ELLINIKA GRAMMATA
ATHENS 2002

CONTENTS

Eggs - Omelets

Vegetables - Legumes

Pasta - Rice

Meat

FISH

PIES

SWEETS

SAUCES

Greek cuisine, yesterday and today

Greek gastronomy and its history is a subject of great international interest as it represents one of the oldest culinary cultures, with a distinctive style and technique. For 2,500 years, Greeks have been savoring the same flavors and dishes created by their ancestors, proving its timeless appeal. Classical Greece is thus the cradle of gastronomy. Like their ancient ancestors, contemporary Greeks do not eat simply to obtain the necessary nourishment for survival. Eating is for enjoyment and in food they seek pleasure. Meals are a ritual for communing, as the ancient Greeks exchanged ideas while sharing a plate of food. Indeed, the Greeks were the first culture to recognize gastronomy as an art form.

Meals in antiquity

In Classical Greece, two meals were taken each day, in contrast to the three meals a day taken in pre-Classical times.

In the Byzantine era, breakfast was known as *ariston*, while the second meal consumed during the day was known as the *deipnon* or, according to Homer, as the *dorpon*.

Breakfast consisted of bread ("a lump of barley for the masses" and "bread of wheat for the rich") dunked in undiluted wine (*akratos oinos*). Greeks considered wine as nourishment and it was even present at the breakfast table.

The ancient Greeks' morning beverage was known as *kykeon*, a mix of wine, grated cheese, and barley flour - to which Circe

Olive Oil

Olive oil is the single most characteristic ingredient of Mediterranean cuisine and immediately comes to mind whenever nutritionists mention the Mediterranean diet.

Many of the amphorae in archaeological collections were used to store olive oil. Olive vats have also been unearthed in several recent excavations, while even older evidence of olive and olive oil

added honey. With breakfast, they also drank milk, mostly from goats, and a beverage made of honey thinned with tepid water. Staples of the breakfast table also included nuts and dried fruit, most commonly dried figs, almonds, and walnuts.

consumption has even been found in Greek caves.

Today, Greece ranks fourth in the production of edible olives and is the third largest producer of olive oil. The olive tree, which has grown in Greece for at least 5,000 years, is a vital part of the economy: about 350,000 families - half of whom live on Crete and in the Peloponnese - earn a living from olive production. Many Greeks also have their own olive groves on their land and are personally involved in growing and producing edible olive oil. Indeed, from November to January, civil servants, private sector workers, and professionals take frequent trips to the provinces for this purpose.

Greeks consume roughly 20 kilos of olive oil per capita each year - a figure that proves which fat pervades their kitchen. Greek cuisine features an incredible variety of recipes whose flavor and body derives from the same basic ingredient: olive oil. Greek olive oil has a delicate flavor and exquisite clarity that enhances rather than overpowers the flavors and colors of the other ingredients used to create each dish, such as vegetables, meat, fish, and even spices.

Foods cooked in olive oil are also quite filling, which is why in Greece they still hold a unique place in the cuisine. The popular saying, "if you don't eat an oily dish, you can't stand up at work" is proof of this point.

Olive oil-based dishes do not use sophisticated culinary tricks but satisfy the appetite simply and deliciously. As for the secret of these dishes, there are two: first, the sauce must be clear and not runny or watery; and, second, tomatoes, when used, should not overpower the other ingredients but let their flavors come through the bright and clear veil of the olive oil.

Vegetables, Fruit, and Spices

The vegetables most commonly sold in the markets of Ancient Greece were cucumbers, artichokes, wild artichokes, peas, pumpkin, broad beans, radishes, beets, garlic, onions, leeks, lettuce, cabbage, wild cabbage, mushrooms, blite or notchweed, marshmallow, wild spinach, asparagus, mustard greens, truffles, nettle, as well as other greens such as celery and wild carrots. Leaves, roots, and blossoms of these plants were all used in cooking.

Fruits consumed in Ancient Greece included apples, wild pears, pears, prunes, cherries, arbutus berries, quince, medlar fruit, mulberries, melons, pomegranates, peaches - which were added to the Greeks' diets later - and, of course, grapes and figs, the two most valuable fruits of the Mediterranean.

The Greeks also consumed dried fruits, such as raisins and dried figs, as well as nuts and seeds such as almonds, walnuts, chestnuts, and linseed.

Legumes and Cereals

Legumes were considered the food of the poor, thus little is known about how they were prepared and eaten in Ancient Greece since such ingredients were not featured in the symposia. The best known legumes were beans, lentils, chickpeas, broad beans, lupines, peas, and a type of puree made from legumes such as fava beans and broad beans.

Cereals were used mainly in the preparation of breads. The poor ate bread made from barley, while bread consumed by the rich was made from wheat. Millet breads were also quite common. Greeks also flavored their bread with spices and other ingredients, such as sesame seeds, mint, fennel, cheese, honey, and, of course, olive oil.

Barley rusks have been part of the Greek diet since antiquity. In Ancient Greece, barley rusks were eaten by the

Meat

Aside from symposia, meat consumption was limited to private and public holidays as sacrifices. The reason was not a trend towards vegetarianism but poverty.

The most commonly consumed meats were rabbit, hare, lamb, boar, wild goat, deer, as well as various fowl (pigeons, patridges, quail, duck, and geese).

Preparation and cooking varied from boiling with

poor, but were also part of the staple diet of the army, sailors, and travelers because they could be preserved for long periods of time. Barley rusks are still popular on Crete and in antiquity were also eaten on other islands such as Santorini, Kimolos, Kassos, and Melos. Foreign travelers who were accustomed to the white French-style loaves of bread viewed these dark rusks with distaste.

vegetables and spices to roast in the oven or on the spit.

Fish

The ancient Greeks have always loved fish, which is why fish consumption was far greater than meat consumption. They ate mainly fatty fish like bogue, whitebait, sardines, chub mackerel, common mackerel, anchovy, eel, and tuna.

The Aegean's fish and seafood is particularly tasty and thus does not need its flavor boosted by sauces or complicated cooking procedures (which actually weaken the natural flavor of the fish). Olive oil and a few delicately-flavored vegetables, fresh tomatoes, okra, celery or aromatic herbs are perfect for enhancing the freshness of the fish.

The healthiest cuisine in the world

It is widely recognized that the Greek cuisine, on which the Mediterranean diet is based, is very beneficial to human health. Numerous studies, from the Seven Countries report to a recent study conducted by Harvard University, confirm that consumption of olive oil and a diet of mostly vegetables, wild greens, fruit, and legumes contribute to the prevention of cardiovascular disease and various oncological illnesses.

For centuries, the ideal nutrient composition of the olive's natural "juice" has been the secret of the health and long lives of the Mediterranean peoples, for whom it is the primary fat source in their daily diet. Its nutritional and biological value to the human body is so great that olive oil is ranked among the top ten

foods. It also contains 600 antioxidant substances, many of which have yet to be fully studied.

Like other oils, olive oil also contains fatty acids, which fall into one of three categories: saturated, polyunsaturated, and monounsaturated. Animal fats contain mostly saturated fats and seed oils mostly polyunsaturated fats. Olive oil differs because it contains up to 83 per cent monounsaturated fat. Other fatty acids in olive oil are traces of saturated fat, and some polyunsaturated fats such as linolic acid, which combined with olive acids give olive oil its unique biological value.

DAKOS WITH OLIVES
(Daki krithini me elyes ke eleolado)

Ingredients

Yield: 6 servings

3 barley dakos (barley rusks)
10 Tbs olive oil
1 cup green olives, pitted and minced
2 Tbs lemon juice
1 tsp grated lemon peel
coarse sea salt

Preparation

1. In mixing bowl, toss olives with grated lemon peel and sea salt.
2. Wet each barley rusk under running water. Set down to drain, then drizzle with generous portions of olive oil.
3. Sprinkle with lemon juice and spread with olive mix. Serve immediately.

DAKOS WITH TOMATO AND FETA
(Dakos krithinos me tomata, feta ke rigani)

Ingredients

Yield: 6 servings

2 double dakos (barley rusks)
1 large ripe tomato
2 Tbs olive oil
2 Tbs feta or sour mizithra, crumbled
1/2 tsp oregano
salt to taste

Preparation

1. Wet dakos by holding briefly under running water or quickly dipping in a bowl of water. Finely chop tomato, or press through grater.
2. Drizzle dakos with half of the olive oil, then season with salt. Spoon tomato pulp over dakos, leaving a well in the center for cheese. Spoon cheese into center.
3. Sprinkle with salt and oregano. Drizzle remaining olive oil over top. Serve.

BAKED FETA
(Feta psiti ston fourno)

Ingredients

Yield: 4 servings

1/2 kilo feta, sliced 1 cm thick and cut into 10 cm squares
1 tsp. oregano
1 tomato, sliced
4 Tbs. olive oil

Preparation

Place each feta square on a piece of aluminum foil large enough to wrap up cheese. Drizzle cheese with olive oil, sprinkle with oregano, and top with a tomato slice. Fold aluminum foil to create a small, sealed packet. Place in oven and heat at 200°C for 20 minutes. Serve hot.

FETA BREAD
(Tiropsomo me feta)

Ingredients
> Yield: 7-10 servings

1/2 kilo white bread dough
2 eggs
200 grams hard feta, crumbled
2-3 Tbs olive oil
2-3 Tbs flour

Preparation
1. Place dough in large mixing bowl. Using your fingers, make a well in the center. Break eggs into the well, then add feta and one tablespoon olive oil. Knead with swift, firm movements until all ingredients have been thoroughly combined with the dough.
2. Add flour and knead until dough is stiff. Separate dough into two or three pieces. Shape each piece into a round loaf; press level with the palm of your hand. Place on oiled baking sheet and bake at 180°C for 45-50 minutes.

STUFFED OLIVE BREAD
(Yemisto elyopsomo)

Ingredients
> Yield: 10 servings

4 cups white flour
15 grams fresh yeast
1 pinch sugar
1 tsp salt
3 eggs
6 tablespoons olive oil

2 tablespoons blanched almonds, finely chopped
1 cup Kalamata olives, pitted
1 bunch fresh parsley, finely chopped
1 1/2 cups grated cheese (Gruyere or mild kefalotiri)

Preparation
1. Dissolve yeast in a little warm water and stir in sugar. Cover with a warm towel and let mixture foam for 15 minutes.
2. Place yeast in large mixing bowl. Add one egg, flour, and olive oil. Knead until dough is smooth and elastic. Sprinkle with flour; cover with a towel and let rise in warm place for about one hour, or until double.
3. In a separate bowl, mince olives. Stir in parsley, grated cheese, and almonds.
4. When dough has risen, divide in two and roll out each piece into a 16x16 cm sheet at least 2 cm thick. Spread 1/2 the olive mix over each piece of dough, then roll each piece into a tight loaf.
5. Line two baking sheets with non-stick paper. Using a sharp knife, slice each loaf. Place each slice on the baking sheet, then lightly press level with the palm of your hand.
6. Beat two eggs, and brush over each slice. Cover with aluminum foil and let rise for 25-30 minutes, or until double.
7. Bake at 200°C for 25-30 minutes.

OLIVE BREAD WITH FETA
(Elyopsomo me feta)

Ingredients

Yield: 10 servings

2 cups all-purpose white flour
5 grams dry yeast
2 Tbs olive oil
1 tsp oregano
10 green olives, pitted
100 grams feta, crumbled
1 small tomato, finely chopped
pinch of salt
pepper

Preparation

1. In large bowl, dissolve yeast with a cup of warm water. Add olive oil, oregano, and olives. Gradually add salt and enough flour to form smooth dough. Cover with a cotton kitchen towel and let rise in warm place until double.
2. Punch down and divide dough in two. Shape each piece into a loaf and sprinkle with feta and tomato. Bake at 180°C for 40 minutes. Eat hot or at room temperature.

OLIVES FRIED IN GARLIC AND THYME
(Elyes tiganites me kremmidi ke thimari)

Ingredients

Yield: 10 servings

2 1/2 cups Thassos-style olives
1 large onion, thinly sliced
1 tsp thyme
1 tsp oregano
1 1/2 cups olive oil

Preparation

1. Soak olives in cool water for 12 hours. Rinse with clean water, strain, and drain on paper towels. Let stand until dry.
2. In large, deep frying pan, heat olive oil. Lightly cook onions but do not brown.
3. Add olives and fry lightly for 4-6 minutes. Turn olives with oil into a sieve and let strain.
4. Sprinkle olives with thyme and oregano. Toss and serve warm or cold. Olives can also be stored in the refrigerator.

CYPRIOT CUPS WITH KALAMATA OLIVES
(Kipriakes koupes me elyes kalamon)

Ingredients

Yield: 7 servings

3 cups bulghur wheat
5 cups water (for soaking wheat)
1 tsp. salt
1/2 cup olive oil
1 potato, boiled and mashed

• For the filling:
12 mushrooms, finely chopped
2 Tbs. pine nuts
2 Tbs. olive oil
1 small onion, minced
10 Kalamata olives, minced
2 Tbs. parsley, minced
2 cups olive oil for frying
salt
pepper

Olive bread with feta and olives fried in garlic and thyme ▶

Preparation
1. Soak wheat in water overnight.
2. The following day, add mashed potato, olive oil, one teaspoon salt, and a little warm water to the soaked wheat. Knead until ingredients are thoroughly combined.
3. In a frying pan, sauté mushrooms and onion in a little olive oil until tender. Add parsley, two tablespoons water; season with pepper and let cook for 8-10 minutes, until all liquid has been absorbed. Set aside; when cool, mix in pine nuts and minced olives.
4. Separate wheat into pieces roughly the size of a large apricot. Roll each piece into an oval, egg-like shape. Wet your finger in a little water and poke a hole into the wheat ball. Push mushroom filling into the center, then seal with wheat mixture.
5. Fry wheat balls in plenty of olive oil. Drain on kitchen paper; serve hot or cool.

POTATO GARLIC DIP
(Skordalia me patates)

Ingredients
Yield: 10 servings
3 medium potatoes, boiled
4 cloves garlic, crushed
1 cup extra virgin olive oil
4 Tbs strong red wine vinegar
salt

Preparation
1. Place garlic and a small quantity of olive oil in blender. Combine at high speed.
2. Feed potatoes into blender, piece by piece. Gradually add olive oil and vinegar; when all the olive oil has been absorbed, taste and, if necessary, correct seasoning by adding salt, pepper, or a little more vinegar.
3. Empty garlic dip into a serving bowl and garnish with 2-3 olives.

GARLIC DIP WITH WALNUTS
(Skordalia me karidia)

Ingredients
Yield: 10 servings
2 slices whole-wheat bread, softened in
water (crusts removed)

5 potatoes, boiled and peeled (warm)
25 walnuts, shelled
7 cloves garlic
olive oil
lemon juice or vinegar
salt
pepper
5-6 black olives

Preparation
1. In blender, combine garlic, salt, pepper, and walnuts. When mix has acquired a paste-like texture, add warm potatoes and bread (after squeezing out water).
2. Gradually add olive oil, alternating with lemon juice or vinegar. Empty into bowl, garnish with olives, and serve.

LEEK TRIANGLES
(Trigona me prassa)

Ingredients
                    Yield: 10-12 servings
1 kilo filo
1 kilo leeks (white part only), finely
    chopped
2 Tbs. butter
1 Tbs. olive oil
2 cups milk
1 cup sweet trahanas
1 cup grated kefalotiri (or other hard
    cheese)
4 eggs, lightly beaten
salt
pepper

Preparation
1. Simmer leeks in one cup milk over medium heat for approximately 25 minutes. Add butter and stir vigorously with wooden spoon until leeks are coated and butter has been absorbed. Add olive oil, trahanas, salt and pepper; reduce heat and simmer until cooked.
2. Remove from heat; stir in cheese and eggs. Cover and set aside to cool.
3. Take two sheets of filo and cut lengthwise into five strips. Lightly brush one strip with olive oil. Place a spoonful of leek mix near the edge of the strip, and then fold diagonally to form a small triangle. Place on lightly buttered cookie sheet. Repeat with remaining leek mixture. Bake at 170°C for 40 minutes, or until golden brown.

PUMPKIN PIES
(Pittakia me kolokitha)

Ingredients
                    Yield: 10 servings
• *For the crust*
1 kilo flour
2 tsp. salt
2 Tbs. olive oil
juice of one-half lemon
water

• *For the filling*
2 1/2 kilos pumpkin
3 eggs, lightly beaten
1 cup olive oil
2 onions, finely chopped
1 1/2 cups grated cheese
1 tsp fresh mint
1 cup olive oil or corn oil for frying

cumin
salt
pepper

Preparation

1. Prepare dough for crust: In large mixing bowl, combine olive oil, lemon juice, and salt. Gradually stir in flour and enough water to form soft dough that is not sticky to the touch.
2. Cut pumpkin into pieces and sauté with onions in olive oil. Stirring gently, cook pumpkin until it is tender and has sweated all its juices. Empty into sieve and strain liquid. Place pumpkin in a mixing bowl and combine with eggs, cheese, cumin, salt, and pepper.
3. Roll out dough into thin sheets. Using pastry cutter or a saucer cut out circles 4-5 cms diameter. Spoon filling onto half the circle, then fold remaining dough over filling to form a semi-circle; pinch sides together with a fork.
4. Fry in hot oil and serve warm.

SPINACH PIES WITH MINT
(Spanakopittakia me diosmo)

Ingredients

Yield: 10-12 servings

• *For the crust*
700 grams flour
1 cup milk
1 cup olive oil
2 eggs
1 tsp salt

• *For the filling*
1 1/2 kilos spinach
1 bunch parsley
6-8 spring onions (green stems only)
2 Tbs. mint, finely chopped
2 cups sour mizithra
1/2 cup olive oil
1 egg, yolk only
salt
pepper
sesame seeds

Preparation

1. On medium speed, use electric mixer to combine eggs, milk, and salt, adding flour gradually to form smooth dough. Turn out onto lightly floured surface and knead gently. Cover with cotton kitchen towel and set aside while preparing filling.
2. Clean spinach; finely chop with parsley. Rub greens with salt until they are limp and deep green.
3. Combine greens with spring onions, mint, pepper, olive oil, and mizithra.
4. Divide dough into pieces and roll out into sheets. Using pastry cutter or saucer cut into circles 7-8 cms in diameter. Spoon some filling onto half the circle, then fold the other half over the filling; pinch dough together with a fork.
5. Brush tops with beaten egg yolk, sprinkle with sesame seeds and bake at 180°C for 20 minutes or until golden brown.

FAVABALLS
(Favatokeftedes)

Ingredients

Yield: 6 servings

2 cups cooked fava
2 Tbs. onion, finely chopped
1 tsp mint
2 Tbs. fine semolina
1 cup olive oil
salt
pepper

Preparation

1. Place fava in large bowl. (Fava should be prepared at least one day ahead and chilled in refrigerator until thick.)
2. Into bowl, add onion, mint, semolina, salt, and pepper. Hand-mix until all ingredients are thoroughly combined.
3. Shape mixture into walnut-sized balls; squeeze firm by cupping in the palm of your hand.
4. Refrigerate for one hour. Add olive oil to non-stick pan and heat.
5. Using slotted spoon, place fava balls in oil and fry over high heat until golden brown.
6. Remove and drain on paper towels. Serve hot.

POTATO BALLS
(Patatokeftedes)

Ingredients

Yield: 6 servings

1 kilo potatoes
2 eggs, lightly beaten
200 grams feta, crumbled
salt
pepper
flour
oil for frying

Preparation

1. Scrub potatoes and boil in their skins.
2. Remove skin and mash. Add parsley, eggs, feta, salt, and pepper. Combine thoroughly.
3. Shape mashed potato mix into walnut-sized balls; roll in flour and fry until golden.

CORIANDER POTATOES
(Patates me koliandro)

Ingredients

Yield: 10 servings

1 1/2 kilo new (or small round)
   potatoes
1 Tbs. coriander, crushed
1/2 cup red wine
salt
pepper

Preparation
1. Scrub and peel potatoes. Fry in hot oil without stirring or moving around.
2. When cooked, remove to shallow saucepan over low heat. Add wine, sprinkle with coriander, and let simmer until liquid has been absorbed. Serve hot.

FRIED PEPPERS WITH YOGURT SAUCE
(Piperies tiganites ke saltsa yiaourtiou)

Ingredients

Yield: 6 servings

12 bell (or green) peppers
1 1/2 cups thick yogurt
3-4 cloves garlic, crushed
2 Tbs. strong red wine vinegar
1 1/2 cups olive oil

Preparation
1. Wash peppers thoroughly. Cut lengthwise and core. Rinse and place in colander to drain.
2. Fry peppers in hot olive oil until soft and lightly browned. Remove with a fork and drain on paper towels. Carefully remove skin and arrange peppers in a spoke pattern around the edge of a round serving platter. Sprinkle with vinegar.
3. Crush garlic with a little salt; thoroughly blend pulp with yogurt, one tablespoon olive oil, and vinegar to taste. Whisk ingredients together until light and creamy. Pour over peppers.
4. Refrigerate for 2-3 hours. Serve cold.

PEPPERS WITH FETA
(Yemistes piperies me feta)

Ingredients

Yield: 8 servings

8 green horn (or chili) peppers
1/2 cup olive oil
1 large onion, grated
1 large tomato, finely chopped
1 Tbs. parsley, minced
200 grams feta, coarsely chopped
olive oil
oregano
ground pepper

Preparation
1. Wash peppers; cut off tops and carefully remove seeds without tearing skin. Poach peppers in boiling water for 5 minutes; drain and set aside to cool.
2. Meanwhile, sauté onions in olive oil. Add tomato, ground pepper, and oregano. Stir and remove from heat.

▲ *Feta-stuffed peppers and fried peppers with yogurt sauce*

Let cool slightly, then stir in feta and parsley.

3. Fill peppers with mixture. Brush peppers with oil then grill or fry, turning until all sides are browned. Serve hot.

ONION PANCAKES
(Kremmidotiganites)

Ingredients

Yield: 10 servings

5 bunches spring onions, minced
1 bunch fennel, minced
1 bunch mint, minced
2 cups fresh spinach, finely chopped
1 tsp salt
1/2 tsp pepper
1 egg
juice of 1 lemon
8-10 Tbs. all-purpose flour
2 cups olive oil for frying

Preparation

1. In mixing bowl, combine green onions, fennel, mint, spinach, and salt. Rub greens together until all liquid has been squeezed out. Drain.
2. To greens, add egg and lemon juice; stir in flour, one tablespoon at a time. Mix ingredients together until they acquire the consistency of a thick batter.
3. In frying pan, heat olive oil. Drop spoonfuls of mixture into hot oil and fry until golden brown on all sides. Remove with slotted spoon and drain on kitchen towel. Serve hot or warm.

TZATZIKI (YOGURT DIP)
(Tzatziki)

Ingredients

Yield: 10 servings

2 medium cucumbers, whole
2 cloves garlic, crushed
4 Tbs. olive oil
1 Tbs. strong vinegar
2 1/2 cups thick yogurt
1 tsp salt

Preparation

1. Grate cucumbers. Place in mixing bowl and add salt. Squeeze liquid from pulp and strain well. Discard liquid.
2. Beat garlic into yogurt, gradually adding olive oil and vinegar. Beat for 2-3 minutes or until all ingredients have been thoroughly combined. Stir in cucumber pulp. Divide into individual serving bowls; refrigerate for 30 minutes, then serve.

SNAILS WITH ROSEMARY
(*Tiganita saliggaria me dendrolivano ke ksidi*)

Ingredients

Yield: 6 servings

20-25 large snails
1/2 cup olive oil
1 level Tbs. salt
3 Tbs. red wine vinegar
1 piece rosemary

Preparation

1. Clean snails, removing shell and membranes from their mouths.
2. Sprinkle half the salt into a frying pan; place snails, mouth-side down, on salt. Put pan on stove and cook gently for 5 minutes without adding water or olive oil.
3. Pour olive oil over snails, then cook for another 5 minutes. Stir with fork; add salt, rosemary, and vinegar.
4. Bring snails to boil, then remove from heat. Serve hot in their sauce.

▼ *Snails cooked in rosemary and vinegar*

31

PORK LIVER WITH ROSEMARY
(Sikoti hirino me dendrolivano)

Ingredients

Yield: 10 servings

1 large pork liver
5-7 pieces rosemary
1 cup flour
1/2 cup vinegar
2 cups olive oil
salt

Preparation

1. Cut liver into medium-sized pieces and rinse under running water. Place in large colander to drain completely.
2. Salt meat and dredge with flour. Pour olive oil into deep, heavy-bottomed frying pan. When oil has heated to boiling, toss in a piece of liver. Fry until golden on all sides then remove. Drain on paper towels.
3. When all liver pieces have been cooked, transfer to bowl and prepare sauce. (Drain oil from pan and wipe clean. Return pan to stove and add one cup olive oil. Heat, then add rosemary. Fry for 2-3 minutes, sprinkle with 1 teaspoon flour, and immediately add vinegar. Stir vigorously with wooden spoon for 2-3 minutes.) Pour sauce over liver, cover, and let steep for at least 15 minutes before serving.

TSILADIA
(Tsiladia)

Ingredients

Yield: 10-12 servings

1 medium pork head
5-6 pork hocks
1/2 kilo pork meat, from the neck
1 cup juice of Seville (bitter) oranges
1 cup lemon juice
2 Tbs. vinegar
2 pieces orange peel
1 tsp pepper
1 tsp cumin
1 Tbs. salt
2-3 bay leaves

Preparation

1. Thoroughly rinse pork head. Wash hocks separately and burn off any hairs from skin. Place pork head, hocks, and neck meat in deep pot filled with salted water. Boil for at least two hours, removing foam with slotted spoon to ensure a clear broth.
2. Using slotted spoon, remove pork and set aside to cool. Bone meat and cut into small pieces.
3. Pour broth into a clean pot. Add meat, juice of bitter oranges, lemon juice, orange peel, vinegar, and half of spices. Boil uncovered for 7-10 minutes.
4. Let broth stand for 10 minutes. Dust bottom of ceramic bowls with cumin and ground pepper. Place a bay leaf on top of spices. Fill bowls with "tsiladia." Let cool 24 hours before refrigerating.

PICKLES IN ASPIC
(Pihti me toursia)

Ingredients

Yield: 10 servings

1 small pork head
3 pork hocks
2 medium onions
1 chili pepper
1 Tbs. capers
3-4 pickles
2 Tbs. pickled carrots, coarsely
    chopped
1/2 cup lemon juice
2 Tbs. vinegar
1 cup white wine
1 tsp grated orange peel
2-3 cloves
3 bay leaves
3-4 pimentos
salt
pepper

Preparation

1. Thoroughly rinse pork and remove any hairs from skin. Fill a large pot with salted water. Add meat. Push cloves into onion. When water begins to boil, add wine, onion, chili pepper, and pimento. Boil over low heat for at least 2 hours.

2. Strain broth in a fine sieve. Let pork cool, then cut into small pieces.

3. Pour broth into a clean pot and add pickled vegetables, grated orange peel, lemon juice, vinegar, salt, and a little fresh ground pepper. Boil for 7 minutes. Taste and correct seasoning by adding salt or lemon, if necessary. Add pork, stir, and boil slowly for 5 minutes more.

4. Let aspic cool for 1 hour. Place bay leaves in the bottom of deep ceramic bowls. Pour partly cooled aspic into bowls. Let cool for at least 24 hours. Refrigerate.

SPETZOFAI
(Spetzofai Piliou)

Ingredients

Yield: 10 servings

1 1/2 kilos pork sausage, cut into small
 pieces
1/2 kilo green peppers, cut into strips
1 kilo ripe tomatoes, grated
1 cup olive oil
salt
pepper

Preparation

1. Fry peppers in 3/4 cup olive oil.
   Add tomatoes, salt and pepper.
   Let simmer over low heat.
2. Fry sausage in remaining olive
   oil. Drain and add to saucepan
   with peppers. Cook for 15 minutes
   more.

▼ *Spetzofai*

▲ *Meze (snacks) for ouzo: beet salad, tzatziki, olives, koukofava*

SALADS

GREEN SALAD
(Prassini salata)

Ingredients

Yield: 8 servings

2 medium cucumbers
4 medium tomatoes
5 lettuce leaves
1 onion
2 small green peppers
150 grams feta
2 Tbs. olive oil
2 Tbs. vinegar
black olives
fresh parsley, chopped

salt
pepper

Preparation

Wash tomatoes and quarter.
Wash cucumbers and slice.
Peel onions and slice. Top and tail
peppers, remove seeds, and slice
into thin strips. Chop lettuce
coarsely. Arrange vegetables in
a deep salad bowl.
Pour olive oil and vinegar over
salad. Season with salt and pepper.
Add feta and olives; sprinkle
with parsley.

▼ *Green salad*

LEGUME SALAD
(Salata me diafora ospria)

Ingredients

Yield: 10 servings

3/4 cup black-eyed beans
3/4 cup small broad beans
3/4 cup chick-peas or garbanzo beans
3/4 cup navy beans
3/4 cup wheat
1 Tbs. salt
1 cup olive oil
1/2 cup lemon juice or vinegar

Preparation
1. Eight hours ahead, place legumes in separate bowls of cold water to soak. Before cooking, rinse under cold running water.
2. In a large pot, boil wheat for 20 minutes. Strain and set aside.
3. In same pot, bring fresh water to boil. Add broad beans, cook for 25 minutes, strain, and set aside.
4. In same pot, bring fresh water to boil. Add chick-peas and beans, cook for 25 minutes, strain and set aside.
5. Fill pot with fresh water and bring to boil. Add salt and legumes plus black-eyed peas. Boil over high heat until all beans are tender.
6. Strain. Pour beans into a deep salad bowl. Toss with olive oil, lemon juice or vinegar. Serve hot.

▲ *Legume salad*

SHRIMP SALAD
(Garidosalata)

Ingredients

Yield: 8 servings

1 kilo medium-sized fresh shrimp
2 artichoke heads, sliced
1 tsp dill, finely chopped
1 spring onion, finely chopped
2 boiled eggs, sliced
olive oil
2 Tbs. strong vinegar
fresh ground green pepper

Preparation
1. Boil shrimp for five minutes in a little salted water. Strain and peel carefully to remove shells, tails, and heads.
2. In a salad bowl, combine shrimp and artichoke, spring onion, and dill. Garnish with eggs.
3. Place olive oil, salt, pepper, and vinegar in screw-top jar.

Shake vigorously until thoroughly blended. Pour over salad.

4. Chill for 20 minutes before serving.

THRACE CABBAGE SALAD
(Lahanosalata Thrakis)

Ingredients

Yield: 8 servings

1/2 small head cabbage
1 small carrot, grated
1 cup pickled cabbage
1/2 tsp red pepper

3-4 Tbs. olive oil
1 Tbs. vinegar
salt

Preparation

1. Rinse pickled cabbage and let drain.
2. Shred fresh cabbage and place in salad bowl. Add pickled cabbage and carrot. Season with pepper. Using two forks, toss ingredients until thoroughly mixed.
3. In screw-top jar, combine olive oil, vinegar, and salt with 1 teaspoon hot water. Shake hard until slightly pale. Dress salad and serve.

▼ *Thrace cabbage salad*

▲ *Artichoke and potato salad*

ARTICHOKE AND POTATO SALAD

(Salata me agginares, patates ke avga)

Ingredients

Yield: 8 servings

3 fresh artichokes
1 large potato, boiled
3 eggs, boiled and quartered
fresh dill, minced
2-3 Tbs. extra virgin olive oil
1 Tbs. vinegar
1 large lemon
salt
pepper

Preparation

1. Trim artichokes to remove outer leaves. Salt and rub with lemon to prevent discoloring.
2. Cut potato into cubes and place in salad bowl. Add artichokes, dill, and eggs. Season with salt and pepper. Dress with olive oil and vinegar. Toss and serve immediately.

ALMOND, DILL, AND YOGURT SALAD

(Salata me amigdala, anitho ke yiaourti)

Ingredients

Yield: 10 servings

1 kilo almonds, blanched
1/2 kilo thick yogurt, strained
1 cup mayonnaise
1 Tbs. dill, minced
1 cup turkey cold cuts, finely chopped
salt

Preparation

1. In a mixing bowl, combine yogurt with mayonnaise; season lightly with salt. Add almonds, dill, and turkey. Mix well until ingredients are thoroughly combined.
2. Using the back of a spoon or spatula, press salad into bowl so that surface is even. Garnish with finely chopped dill and chill in refrigerator for 2-3 hours before serving.

GARLICKY SPINACH SALAD WITH YOGURT
(Salata me yiaourti, skordo ke spanaki)

Ingredients

Yield: 6 servings

2 cups spinach, finely chopped
1 1/2 cups thick yogurt
1 Tbs. olive oil
2 cloves garlic, finely chopped
1 Tbs. vinegar
salt

Preparation
1. Rinse spinach under cold running water. In a small bowl, whisk together olive oil, vinegar, garlic, salt, and yogurt.
2. Place spinach in salad bowl and dress with yogurt sauce. Refrigerate for at least one hour before serving.

ZUCCHINI SALAD WITH YOGURT DRESSING
(Kria salata me kolokithakia ke yiaourti)

Ingredients

Yield: 8 servings

1 kilo small zucchini (courgettes), grated
3 cloves garlic, crushed
1 cup thick yogurt
1 Tbs. dill, finely chopped
2 Tbs. lemon juice
salt
pepper

Preparation
1. In large mixing bowl, toss raw grated zucchini with salt, pepper, lemon juice, garlic, and dill.
2. Add yogurt and mix thoroughly. Empty into serving bowl; garnish with olives and chill. Serve as accompaniment to grilled or barbecued meat or meatballs.

BEET SALAD WITH YOGURT DRESSING
(Pantzaria salata me yiaourti)

Ingredients

Yield: 8 servings

450 grams beets, boiled
4 Tbs. onion, finely chopped
2 Tbs. parsley, minced
2 Tbs. olive oil
2 tsp. lemon juice or vinegar
salt
freshly ground pepper
3/4 cup thick yogurt

Preparation
1. Peel and cube beets. In a clean bowl, toss beets with remaining ingredients and refrigerate for at least one hour before serving.

BEET SALAD WITH GARLIC
(*Pantzaria salata me skordo*)

Ingredients

Yield: 8 servings

1 kilo small beets
1/2 cup olive oil
1/4 cup vinegar
1 clove garlic, crushed
salt

Preparation
1. Chop greens off beets. Rinse both under running water. Place beets in saucepan, cover with water and boil. Just before beets are done, add greens and cook until beets are tender. Greens should not be mushy.
2. Drain. Separate beets and greens. Skin beets, slice, and arrange with boiled greens on platter.
3. In small mixing bowl, whisk olive oil and vinegar until blended. Pour over salad and let marinade for a few hours before serving.

▼ *Beet salad*

BLACK-EYED PEA SALAD
(*Mavromattika fassolia salata*)

Ingredients

Yield: 8 servings

1/2 kilo black-eyed peas
2 spring onions, thinly sliced
1 medium onion, finely chopped
2 Tbs. capers
5-6 black olives
1 bunch parsley, minced
1 Tbs. dill, minced
5-6 Tbs. olive oil
2 Tbs. vinegar
salt
pepper

Preparation
1. Soak blackeyed peas in cold water for six hours. Strain and add to pot with boiling water. Cook for five minutes. Drain; place in pot with fresh water and boil for approximately 40 minutes.
2. Remove from heat, drain, and let cool. Toss with remaining ingredients, reserving olives for garnish. Serve.

BEAN SALAD
(Fassolakia piaz)

Ingredients

Yield: 8 servings

1/4 kilo dried beans
3 spring onions, finely chopped
1 small onion, sliced
parsley
6-7 black olives
70 grams olive oil
3 Tbs. vinegar
salt
pepper

Preparation
1. Soak beans in water overnight.
2. Drain beans. Place in saucepan, cover with water, and boil for 30 minutes. Drain. Rinse pot, add beans, cover with fresh water, and boil until tender.
3. Drain and let cool slightly. Place in salad bowl; toss with onions. Pour olive oil and vinegar over beans; season with salt and pepper. Garnish with parsley and black olives; serve.

BLACK-EYED PEA AND SPINACH SALAD
(Zesti salata me mavromattika fassolia ke spanaki)

Ingredients

Yield: 8 servings

2 1/2 cups black-eyed peas
1 kilo fresh spinach
7-8 Tbs. olive oil
salt
lemon juice
coarsely ground pepper

Preparation
1. Soak black-eyed peas in cold water for six hours. Drain; add to pot with boiling water and cook for 5 minutes. Strain; rinse pot, add fresh water and bring black-eyed peas back to boil. Cook for 20-25 minutes.
2. Wash and clean spinach, removing hard stems. Chop coarsely. Add chopped spinach to black-eyed peas and boil together for 6-7 minutes more.
3. Remove from heat. With slotted spoon, remove spinach and black-eyed peas from pot and arrange on serving platter. Combine lemon juice, salt, pepper, and olive oil in a screw-top jar and shake hard until thoroughly blended. Pour over warm black-eyed peas and spinach; serve immediately.

YOGURT SALAD
(Yiaourtosalata me toursi ke skordo)

Ingredients

Yield: 8 servings

1 kilo yogurt
3 cloves garlic, crushed
2 cucumbers
1 radish
5-6 pickles
1 Tbs. capers
1 Tbs. parsley, minced
1/2 cup olive oil
salt

• For garnish:
Boiled eggs
Radishes
Olives

Preparation
1. Peel cucumbers and cut into cubes. Finely chop pickles and radish.
2. In large mixing bowl, combine yogurt with olive oil, garlic, and a little salt. Add cucumbers, pickles, radish, capers, and parsley and stir vigorously until thoroughly mixed.
3. Pour mixture into round serving dish. Garnish with slices of hard-boiled egg, radishes, and olives. Chill in refrigerator before serving.

LETTUCE SALAD
(Maroulosalata)

Ingredients

Yield: 4 servings

1 head lettuce
2 spring onions, sliced
1/2 bunch fresh dill, minced
olive oil
lemon juice or vinegar
salt

Preparation
1. Wash lettuce. Let drain, then chop.
2. Place lettuce in salad bowl. Toss with spring onions and dill. A few minutes before serving, combine olive oil, vinegar or lemon juice in a screw-top jar; dress salad, season with salt and serve.

POTATO SALAD
(Patatosalata)

Ingredients

Yield: 8 servings

3 large potatoes, boiled
1 large onion, sliced
1 spring onion, chopped
2-3 pickles, chopped
2 hard-boiled eggs, quartered
1 Tbs. fresh parsley, minced
4-5 black olives
dash of cumin
salt
pepper

Preparation
1. In large bowl, toss potatoes with onions, pickle, cumin, salt, and pepper.
2. Turn into serving bowl. Garnish with boiled eggs and olives. Serve at room temperature or chilled.

EGGS - OMELETS

BAKED OMELET
(Omeleta tou fournou)

Ingredients

Yield: 6 servings

1/2 kilo small zucchini (courgettes)
1/2 kilo potatoes
12 eggs
2 Tbs. parsley
3 tomatoes
2 onions
2 Tbs. mint
3 Tbs. olive oil
salt
pepper

Preparation

1. Wash zucchini and cut into thin slices. Wash and peel potatoes; cut into thin slices. Arrange zucchini and potatoes in layers in a baking pan. Season with salt and pepper, then sprinkle with minced parsley and mint.
2. Heat olive oil in a frying. Gently sauté finely chopped onions for 3-4 minutes. Add tomato, chopped into cubes. Cook gently for 10 minutes. Pour sauce over vegetables in baking pan.
3. Beat eggs with a pinch of a salt and a few drops of water. Pour over vegetables. Shake pan to distribute eggs evenly. Bake at 180°C for 60-65 minutes.

ARTICHOKE OMELET
(Omelletta me agginares)

Ingredients

Yield: 6 servings

2 artichoke heads (preferably wild artichokes), thinly sliced
5 large eggs
2 Tbs. olive oil
salt
freshly ground pepper

Preparation

1. Heat olive oil in heavy-bottomed, non-stick pan. Add artichokes and reduce heat. Gently cook artichokes in oil for about 10 minutes, turning occasionally to make sure artichokes are cooked through.
2. When golden brown, drain about half the olive oil from the pan. Beat eggs with salt, then pour eggs over artichokes.
3. Turn up heat slightly, and cook for 5-6 minutes making sure to turn the omelet at least two or three times so that it is evenly cooked.
4. Serve hot with plenty of fresh ground pepper.

POTATO OMELET
(Omelletta me patates)

Ingredients

Yield: 6 servings

1 large potato
4 eggs
1/2 cup olive oil
salt
pepper

Preparation
1. Peel potato, rinse, and cut lengthwise into long, thin pieces. Heat olive oil in pan and fry potatoes until very lightly browned. In mixing bowl, beat eggs and salt until foamy. Remove potatoes from pan with slotted spoon and let drain on paper towels. Drain about 1/2 olive oil from frying pan. Add potatoes to eggs and toss together; tip mixture back into frying pan.
2. Let omelet set and brown on one side. Slide onto dish or pan lid, and then flip into pan to brown on the other side. Serve hot, cut into pieces and lightly sprinkled with pepper.

SPINACH OMELET
(Omeleta me spanaki)

Ingredients

Yield: 8 servings

1 kilo spinach
7 eggs
3-4 Tbs. olive oil

◀ *Potato omelet and fried eggs with tomatoes*

salt
pepper

Preparation
1. Clean spinach, wash, and chop. Place in pot and let cook in its own liquid. (Do not add water).
2. Remove from heat; turn into colander and squeeze out liquid. In shallow saucepan, sauté spinach in olive oil. Add lightly beaten eggs. Season with salt and pepper.
3. When eggs have been set, use plate to turn omelet. Cook on other side, remove from heat, and serve hot.

EGGPLANT OMELET
(Omeleta me melitzanes)

Ingredients

Yield: 8 servings

3 medium eggplants
6 eggs
3/4 cup grated hard, salty cheese
5-6 Tbs. olive oil
salt
pepper

Preparation
1. Wash eggplants and slice thinly. Salt and let stand for one hour to drain their liquids.
2. Rinse eggplants and let drain their liquids. Fry in olive oil over low heat.
3. Lightly beat eggs; add cheese, salt, and pepper. Pour egg mix over eggplants. When bottom is set, use plate to turn omelet. Cook on other side, remove from heat and serve hot.

ROLLED OMELETS WITH FRESH MINT AND GOAT CHEESE
(Mikres omellettes tilihtes me fresko diosmo ke katsikisio tiri)

Ingredients

Yield: 6 servings

10 eggs
5 Tbs. hard spicy goat cheese
2 1/2 Tbs. fresh mint, finely chopped
2 Tbs. flour
5 Tbs. olive oil
salt
pepper

Preparation

1. In large mixing bowl, beat eggs with wire whisk until foamy. Add flour, cheese, mint, pepper, and pinch of salt.
2. Using fork, stir mixture with circular motions until ingredients bind together.
3. In medium-sized frying pan, heat one tablespoon olive oil. Pour about 1 1/2 cups of mixture into pan, cover, and let cook on one side for about 3 minutes. Flip and cook other side.
4. Remove from pan, roll, and place in serving dish lined with lettuce leaves. Repeat with remaining egg mixture.

CHEESE OMELET
(Omeleta me tiri)

Ingredients

Yield: 6 servings

6 eggs
1/2 cup kefalotiri cheese, grated
2 Tbs. butter
minced parsley
salt
pepper

Preparation

Beat eggs with a fork until frothy. Add cheese, milk, parsley, salt, and pepper. Heat butter in a frying pan. Pour in egg mixture. Cook omelet on both sides. Serve hot.

FRIED EGGS AND TOMATOES
(Avga tiganita sto eleolado me tomata)

Ingredients

Yield: 4 servings

6 Tbs. virgin olive oil
1 large ripe tomato, peeled and rubbed
   through grater
4 eggs
salt
pepper

Preparation

1. Heat non-stick frying pan. Add tomato, season lightly with salt, and let simmer for 6-7 minutes until all liquid has evaporated. Add olive oil and cook gently for 2-3 minutes.
2. One by one, break eggs into pan, lightly sprinkle with pepper, and cook gently for 2-3 minutes while spooning sauce over yolks. Remove from heat and serve.

"CAYIANAS"
(Kayianas)

Ingredients

Yield: 3 servings

3 medium ripe tomatoes, pressed
   through grater
3 eggs
2 onions, finely chopped
4 Tbs. olive oil
pepper

Preparation

1. Brown onions in olive oil. Add tomatoes; let cook until liquid has evaporated.
2. In a bowl, beat eggs with fork. Add tomato mix and beat continuously until eggs set. Serve immediately.

BAKED EGGPLANT
(Melitzanes sto fourno me kima)

Ingredients

Yield: 6 servings

5 round eggplants
1 cup olive oil
1/2 kilo ground beef or lamb
1 medium onion, minced
1 small tomato, minced or 1 Tbs. tomato
    paste
1 tsp. parsley, minced
1 tsp. cumin
salt
pepper

Preparation
1. Top eggplants and cut in half. Fill a cooking pot with boiling water; add one tablespoon olive oil. Immerse eggplant pieces in boiling water for 5 minutes.
2. Using slotted spoon, remove eggplant pieces from pot; set aside to drain. When cool, use a teaspoon to gently scoop out seeds and some flesh. Set eggplant boats aside and prepare filling: heat about half the olive oil and sauté onion for 2-3 minutes; add ground meat, and brown for 4-5 minutes; stir in parsley, salt, pepper, cumin, and one cup water; cover and simmer for 15 minutes.
3. Arrange eggplant boats in a baking pan, skin side down. Spoon stuffing into each boat. Top with tomato, then drizzle with olive oil. Add one-half cup water to pan. Place in oven and bake at 180°C for 30-35 minutes. Serve warm.

EGGPLANT BOATS WITH CHEESE
(Melitzanes varkoules me tiri)

Ingredients

Yield: 10 servings

2 kilos eggplant, preferably long variety
1/2 cup olive oil, plus some extra for
    brushing vegetables
2 medium onions, finely chopped
2 cups kefalotiri, grated (may substitute
    any hard, salty cheese)
2 Tbs. cornstarch
1 cup milk
1/2 cup dry breadcrumbs
1/2 cup parsley, minced
2 eggs, beaten
salt
pepper

Preparation
1. Wash and top eggplant. Cut lengthwise down the middle, scald, and drain carefully, taking care to keep the eggplant pieces whole. Let cool, then scoop out flesh without breaking skin. Set eggplant skin "boats" aside.
2. In a deep frying pan, heat oil and braise onions. Puree eggplant flesh

in vegetable mill and add to frying pan. Let cook over low heat for about 5 minutes, stirring vigorously.

3. Combine cornstarch with milk. Pour mixture into frying pan, and beat with wood spoon until it begins to thicken. Remove from heat. Let cool, then add remaining ingredients. Stir until thoroughly mixed. Spoon mixture into eggplant skins and place side by side in baking dish. Bake at 200°C for 45 minutes, until golden brown. Serve hot or cold.

ARTICHOKES A LA POLITA
(Agginares a la Polita)

Ingredients

Yield: 6 servings

2 kilos artichokes
juice of 1 1/2 lemons
1 cup olive oil
1-2 Tbs. flour
2 medium lemons
3 small potatoes, whole
6 small onions, whole
5 spring onions, finely chopped
3 Tbs. dill, finely chopped

▲ *Artichokes a la Polita*

2-3 carrots, sliced into rounds
salt
pepper

Preparation
1. Fill large mixing bowl with water. Add juice of 1/2 lemon and flour.
2. Wash and clean artichokes: cut off stem, leaving about one inch of stalk, pull off exterior leaves, trim thorny tops, and scoop out fuzzy "choke" in center of artichoke.
3. Rub artichokes with lemon and let soak in the lemon-water.
4. In large saucepan over high heat, cook olive oil, onions, spring onions, dill, carrots, potatoes, artichoke stalks, salt, pepper, juice of 1 1/2 lemons, and two cups water.
5. Rinse artichokes and place in saucepan. Lower heat, and let boil until all water has been absorbed.
6. To avoid discoloration, cover artichokes while cooking and don't open lid often.

ARTICHOKES WITH PEAS
(Agginares me araka)

Ingredients
Yield: 8 servings

6 medium artichokes
1/2 kilo peas
250 grams spring onions
1 bunch dill, minced
100 grams olive oil
juice of one lemon
salt
pepper

Preparation
1. Clean artichoke, removing stem and hard outer leaves. Trim ends of artichoke heads and quarter. Scoop out fuzzy "choke" and place artichoke quarters in a bowl of water with juice of one lemon to prevent discoloration.
2. Brown onions in olive oil until tender. Add peas, strained artichokes, and two cups water; season with salt and pepper and bring to boil. Cook for 20-25 minutes. Serve hot.

VEGETABLES STUFFED WITH RICE AND BEEF
(Yemista lahanika me rizi ke kima)

Ingredients
Yield: 6 servings

5 medium-sized tomatoes
3 zucchinis (courgettes)
2 eggplants (aubergines)
3 bell (green) peppers
20-30 grapevine leaves
3 large onions, finely chopped
1/2 kilo ground beef
1 bunch parsley, finely chopped
1 tsp. oregano
1 1/2 cups rice
1 1/2 cups olive oil
1 tsp. salt
1 tsp. black pepper
pinch of cumin

Preparation
1. Brown onions and ground beef in olive oil. Simmer for 6-7 minutes,

Artichokes with peas and stewed okra ▶

stirring with fork to prevent meat from clumping.

2. Season with salt, pepper, and cumin. Add rice and let simmer for 8-10 minutes more.

3. Scoop out pulp from tomatoes, zucchinis, eggplant, and peppers. Salt and set aside to drain liquids.

4. Let meat mixture cool slightly and then add vegetable pulp, oregano, parsley, and dill. Stir well with spoon or mix together by hand.

5. Spoon filling into vegetable shells and wrap in grapevine leaves. Place stuffed vegetables and grapevine leaf rolls side by side in baking dish; drizzle with olive oil and lightly season with salt. Cover with aluminum foil or a layer of vine leaves. Bake at 180°C for 50-60 minutes. Serve warm or at room temperature.

CAULIFLOWER WITH EGG-LEMON SAUCE
(Kounoupidi avgolemono)

Ingredients

Yield: 8 servings

1 cauliflower (roughly 1 kilo)
1 large onion, finely chopped
1 bay leaf
1 cup olive oil
1/2 cup white wine
1 egg
1 medium-sized lemon
3 pimentos or pinch of cumin
salt
pepper

Preparation

1. Wash cauliflower under running water. Chop into pieces and blanch in boiling water for 5 minutes. Remove with slotted spoon and place in colander to drain.

2. Pour olive oil into saucepan. Fry onion in olive oil for 2-3 minutes until it begins to brown slightly. Add cauliflower, turning with fork until all pieces have been coated and glisten. Add wine, two cups water, bay leaf, pimento, and salt. Cover and let cook over high heat for 10 minutes.

3. Turn off heat. In glass heat-proof mixing bowl, beat egg. Still whisking, slowly add lemon juice, alternating with warm broth from the saucepan.

4. Remove pan from heat. Tip egg-lemon-broth mixture into pan and stir gently. Serve warm, with freshly ground pepper.

CAULIFLOWER CASSEROLE
(Kounoupidi yiahni)

Ingredients

Yield: 8 servings

1 kilo cauliflower
2 large fresh tomatoes, chopped into pulp
1/2 tsp. tomato paste
1 large onion, finely chopped
1 sprig parsley
3/4 cup olive oil
3 pimentos
1 cinnamon stick
salt
freshly ground pepper

Preparation
1. Wash cauliflower and trim, keeping tender florets and discarding tough part of stalk.
2. Sauté onion in olive oil for 4-5 minutes. Add cauliflower and 1 cup water.
3. Cover saucepan and cook over high heat for 10 minutes.
4. Add tomato, parsley, spices, and one cup water. Cook until cauliflower is tender.
5. Remove cinnamon stick. Serve cauliflower in its sauce, hot or warm.

BLITE CASSEROLE
(Blita me skordo yiahni)

Ingredients

Yield: 8 servings

1 kilo blite (or other greens)
2 medium potatoes, quartered
3 cloves garlic, halved

1 large ripe tomato, cubed
1 large onion, finely chopped
1/2 cup olive oil
pinch of cumin
3-4 drops lemon juice
salt
pepper

Preparation
1. In a deep saucepan, brown onion in olive oil for 2-3 minutes. Add coarsely chopped greens and sauté for 5-7 minutes more. Add potatoes, garlic, tomato, and two cups water. Cover and cook for 25 minutes.
2. With fork, stir in cumin, salt, pepper, and a few drops of lemon juice. Cook for 10 minutes more.
3. Serve hot or at room temperature.

BAKED BEANS WITH GREENS
(Yigantes sto fourno me hortarika)

Ingredients

Yield: 8 servings

1 kilo spinach
500 grams large, dried flageolet (or broad) beans
1 small leek, finely chopped
1 Tbs. dill
3 spring onions, finely chopped
1 cup hard feta cheese, crumbled
2 ripe tomatoes, finely chopped
1 cup olive oil
salt
pepper
dry breadcrumbs

Preparation
1. Soak beans in water overnight. Boil until half-cooked, then drain.
2. Wash and trim spinach. Chop coarsely. Drain in colander and rub with salt to draw out liquids.
3. Wring spinach dry. Chop leek, spring onions, and dill; add to spinach along with half of the feta.
4. Spread half of the mixture in bottom of baking dish. Place beans on top, then layer remaining spinach mix over beans.
5. Cover with oil, tomatoes (pulp and juice), and remaining feta. Sprinkle pepper and breadcrumbs or fine semolina on top. Bake in medium oven for approximately one hour.

▲ *Baked beans with greens*

VEGETARIAN GRAPEVINE LEAF ROLLS
(*Nistissima dolmadakia*)

Ingredients

Yield: 6 servings

50-60 grapevine leaves
1 1/2 cups rice
7-8 spring onions, finely chopped
1 small onion, finely chopped
1 Tbs. mint, finely chopped
2 large tomatoes, chopped into a pulp
1 cup olive oil
juice of one large lemon
salt
pepper

Preparation
1. In saucepan, heat 1/2 cup olive oil. Sauté onions and rice for approximately 5 minutes, stirring continuously.
2. Add tomato and mint. Season with salt and pepper. Let filling cook over low heat for 5-6 minutes. Remove from stove.
3. When filling is cool, spoon a small amount onto a grapevine leaf. Place filling near the edge, then roll leaf tight.
4. Arrange stuffed, rolled grapevine leaves in layers along the bottom of a deep saucepan, working from the outer edge of the pan towards the center. Pour 1/2 cup olive oil and one cup water over the grapevine rolls. Cover and simmer for 45-50 minutes.
5. Serve warm or at room temperature.

▲ Dolmades (stuffed vine leaves)

STUFFED TOMATOES
(Tomates yemistes me rizi)

Ingredients

Yield: 6 servings

6 large, ripe tomatoes
8-9 Tbs. short-grain rice
4 large onions, finely chopped
1 large bunch parsley, finely chopped
2 carrots, shredded
2 zucchinis (courgettes), shredded
1 artichoke head, shredded
1 cup olive oil
1 tsp. sugar
1/2 tsp. oregano
salt
pepper

7-8 large grapevine leaves
1 cup olive oil for baking pan

Preparation

1. Slice tops off tomatoes; carefully scoop out pulp. Reserve tops and pulp. Sprinkle hollowed-out tomatoes with salt and set upside down to drain.

2. In large mixing bowl, combine 1 cup olive oil, tomato pulp, onions, carrots, artichoke, zucchinis, parsley, rice, oregano, sugar, salt, and pepper. Mix well with your hand. Mixture should be slightly watery.

3. Spoon mixture into tomato shells. Cover each tomato with its own lid. Place tomatoes in baking pan and

cover with grapevine leaves to prevent burning.

4. Over grapevine leaves, grate one large ripe tomato. Cover with one cup olive oil. Place baking pan in oven. Cook at 150°C for approximately 30 minutes. When half-cooked, remove grapevine leaves and continue baking until tomato skins are nicely browned. Serve warm or at room temperature.

BAKED EGGPLANT WITH FETA
(Melitzanes me feta sto fourno)

Ingredients
                        Yield: 8-10 servings
3 large eggplants
3 large tomatoes, peeled and finely chopped
3 large onions, finely chopped
1 clove garlic, crushed
2 Tbs. parsley, minced
1 kilo hard feta cheese, thinly sliced
olive oil for frying
salt
pepper

Preparation
1. Wash and top eggplants. Slice into thin rounds. Soak slices in cool, salted water for 25-30 minutes to remove bitter taste. Strain.
2. Fry eggplant slices in olive oil but do not brown. Drain on paper towels.
3. Prepare light sauce by combining tomatoes, parsley, onions, and a little olive oil.
4. Line bottom of small, oven-proof

dish with one layer of fried eggplant slices. Top with one layer of sauce and one layer of feta. Repeat, reserving a little sauce to spoon over last feta layer.

5. Bake at 180°C for 40 minutes. Let cool slightly, then cut into squares and serve.

HANIA "BOUREKI"
(Boureki Haniotiko)

Ingredients
                        Yield: 8 servings
1/2 kilo zucchini (courgettes) or yellow squash
4 medium potatoes
1 kilo sweet mizithra (or any soft goat cheese)
1/2 kilo hard feta cheese, grated
1 cup yogurt, strained
2 medium tomatoes, finely chopped
4 Tbs. light cream
1 Tbs. fresh mint, finely chopped
3 Tbs. olive oil
2 cups flour
pinch of salt
pepper

Preparation
1. Cut potatoes and zucchini into very thin slices. Transfer to a large bowl and salt lightly. In separate bowl, combine cheeses until thoroughly blended. To zucchini, add tomatoes, mint, half the cheese mix, cream, olive oil, pepper, and 1 1/2 cups flour. Using your hands, knead mixture until all ingredients are thoroughly combined.

2. Transfer mixture to a lightly oiled baking pan. Use spatula to distribute into an even layer. Spread remaining cheese mix over top; sprinkle with remaining flour.
3. Bake at 200°C for 45 minutes. Cover with aluminum foil and bake at 150°C for 30 minutes more. Serve at room temperature or cool.

STUFFED STOVE-TOP EGGPLANT
(Melitzanes stin katsarola yemistes me kefalotiri i graviera)

Ingredients
Yield: 6 servings
6 eggplants (thin, elongated variety)
1/4 kefalotiri or gruyere cheese
2 medium ripe tomatoes, pressed through grater
3 cloves garlic
2 large onions, finely chopped
1 cup olive oil
salt
pepper

Preparation
1. Wash and top eggplants. Dissolve one teaspoon salt and one-half teaspoon sugar in large bowl of cool water. Soak eggplants for two hours to remove bitterness.
2. Slice eggplants lengthwise but do not separate. Lightly salt flesh. Insert one piece of cheese, one clove garlic and a little onion into eggplant.
3. Heat olive oil in a large, heavy-bottomed saucepan. Lightly brown remaining onions. Arrange eggplants in saucepan, cut side up.
4. Pour tomato over eggplants; season with pepper, then add one cup water. Cover pot and cook over medium heat for 50 minutes. Remove; sprinkle with grated cheese and serve hot.

POTATO STEW
(Patates me kremmidakia)

Ingredients
Yield: 8 servings
1/2 kilo small whole potatoes (or large potatoes cut into pieces)
1/2 kilo stewing onions (small, whole bulbs)
2-3 tomatoes (or 1 can stewed tomatoes)
1/2 cup red wine
1 Tbs. vinegar
3 Tbs. olive oil
1 bay leaf
oregano
pinch of cinnamon
pinch of cumin
salt
pepper
water, as needed

Preparation
1. Clean onions and potatoes. Sauté in olive oil; add seasonings, then pour over wine and vinegar.
2. Add tomatoes, a little water; correct seasoning. Cook slowly, adding enough water to keep potatoes moist. Remove from heat when potatoes are cooked through and thick sauce has formed.

POTATO CASSEROLE
(Patates yiahni)

Ingredients

Yield: 6 servings

1 kilo medium potatoes
2 medium onions, grated
1 large ripe tomato, crushed
1/2 cup olive oil
1 clove garlic, minced
1 Tbs. parsley, minced

Preparation

1. Wash potatoes, remove skin, and cut into pieces. Lightly brown onion and garlic in olive oil.
2. Add potatoes and stir gently with a spoon. Add 2 1/2 cups water. Cover and let simmer for 15 minutes.
3. Remove cover. Add tomato, parsley, salt, and pepper. Cook for 20 minutes more or until all liquids, except oil, have evaporated and potatoes are tender. Serve warm or at room temperature.

"BRIAM"
(Briam)

Ingredients

Yield: 8 servings

400 grams potatoes
350 grams eggplant
350 grams zucchini
400 grams tomato
3 medium onions
1 Tbs. parsley
100 grams olive oil
salt
pepper

Preparation

1. Peel potatoes and onions; slice. Wash remaining vegetables and cut into bite-sized pieces.
2. In a cooking pot, arrange vegetables in layers, with onions as bottom layer and zucchini as top layer. Season with salt and pepper.
3. Pour olive oil and one cup water over vegetables. Cover and cook over medium heat for about one hour. Remove; sprinkle each serving with minced parsley.

MACARONI AND LEEK CASSEROLE
(Pastitsio me prassa)

Ingredients

Yield: 10 servings

1/2 kilo Greek macaroni (thick, hollow spaghetti)
2 kilos leeks
3/4 cup olive oil
2 tomatoes
1 cup whole-fat yogurt
1 clove garlic
1 cup gruyere cheese, grated

Preparation

1. Boil pasta; strain. Toss with half the olive oil. Slice leeks, boil, and strain. Toss with remaining olive oil. In blender, combine yogurt, tomatoes, and garlic.
2. In lightly oiled baking dish, layer half the pasta along bottom. Top with leeks. Layer remaining pasta over vegetables. Pour blended tomatoes and yogurt over top.

Sprinkle with grated cheese. Bake in medium oven until top is golden brown.

STEWED OKRA
(Bamyes laderes)

Ingredients

Yield: 6 servings

1/2 kilo okra, fresh or frozen
4 large ripe tomatoes (or 1 can stewed tomatoes)
1/2 cup olive oil
1 large onion, finely chopped
juice of one lemon or 2 Tbs. vinegar
salt
pepper

Preparation
1. If using fresh okra, top and cut in two if large. Rinse and strain in colander.
2. Pour lemon juice over okra and let stand for about one-half hour until vegetables drain their liquids.
3. Sauté onions in olive oil. Add okra, tomatoes, salt, pepper, a few drops of lemon juice, and one cup of water. Cover and simmer for 20-25 minutes.

Legumes

BAKED BEANS
(Yigantes ston fourno)

Ingredients

Yield: 8 servings

1 cup plus 2 Tbs. olive oil
2 cups large flageolet (or broad) beans, soaked in water for 7-8 hours
2 onions, finely chopped
1 bunch celery leaves, finely chopped
2 cloves garlic, slivered
1 tsp. tomato paste
1 large ripe tomato, crushed
1 medium tomato, sliced
1 tsp. oregano
1/2 tsp. cumin
3-4 drops lemon juice
1 tsp. sugar
salt
pepper

Preparation
1. Boil beans for 25 minutes in plenty of water. Drain thoroughly.
2. Heat olive oil in saucepan. Add onion and garlic; cook until lightly browned (approximately 3-4 minutes). Add tomato pulp, tomato paste diluted in one cup water, spices, sugar, and lemon. Stir, then add another cup water. Cover and simmer for 15-20 minutes.
3. Empty beans into baking dish. Pour sauce over beans. Arrange tomato slices over top in a pretty design and sprinkle with pepper. Bake at 180°C for 30-40 minutes.
4. Serve hot or at room temperature.

BEAN SOUP
(Fasolada soupa)

Ingredients

Yield: 8 servings

1/2 kilo dried beans
250 grams olive oil
1 red chili pepper (optional)
3 large ripe tomatoes, pressed through
    grater
2 carrots, sliced
2 medium onions, finely chopped
1/2 bunch of leaf celery, finely chopped
salt
pepper

Preparation
1. Soak beans overnight.
2. The next day, rinse and boil in
    ample water for about 10 minutes.
    Strain, rinse, and place in pot with
    fresh water. Boil with onions for
    about 20 minutes.
3. Add carrots and celery. Bring to
    boil. Next add tomatoes and chili
    pepper; boil for 60-90 minutes
    more.
4. About 15 minutes before removing
    from heat, stir in olive oil, salt and
    pepper. When done, let beans rest
    for 20 minutes before serving.

CHICKPEAS IN TOMATO SAUCE
(Revithia me saltsa tomatas)

Ingredients

Yield: 8 servings

1/2 kilo chickpeas
3 large ripe tomatoes, pressed through
    grater
1 onion, finely chopped
1/2 cup olive oil
salt
pepper
cumin

Preparation
1. Soak chickpeas overnight. The next
    day, strain and set aside. In
    saucepan, sauté onions in oil. Add
    chickpeas and water to cover; boil
    for 30-40 minutes.
2. Add tomato, salt, cumin, and
    pepper; boil for 20 minutes more.
    Serve hot.

▲ *Chick-pea soup*

CHICKPEA SOUP WITH LEMON JUICE
(Revithia soupa me himmo apo lemoni)

Ingredients

Yield: 8 servings

1 cup virgin olive oil
2 cups chickpeas (or garbanzo beans), soaked in water for 7-8 hours
1 large onion, grated
1/2 cup lemon juice
1 tsp. flour
salt
pepper

Preparation
1. Boil chickpeas for 10 minutes in plenty of water. Drain.
2. Sauté onion in hot olive oil for 3-4 minutes. Add chickpeas and stir. Add 8-9 cups water. Cover and cook for 30-45 minutes. Season with salt and pepper to taste.
3. Mix flour with lemon juice and add to chickpeas. Boil without lid for 10 minutes. Serve hot or at room temperature.

LENTIL SOUP
(Fakes soupa)

Ingredients

Yield: 8 servings

2 cups lentils
3 large ripe tomatoes, pressed through grater
2 cloves garlic, thinly sliced
2 bay leaves
1 large onion, finely chopped
2 carrots, cleaned and sliced
3-4 Tbs. red wine vinegar
3/4 cup olive oil
salt
pepper
vinegar for serving

Preparation
1. Clean lentils; place in pot with ample water and bring to boil. Let boil for a few minutes, then strain. Fill pot with fresh water, add lentils, return to heat and boil for about 20 minutes.
2. Add garlic, onions, carrots, bay leaves and continue cooking. When lentils are slightly tender, add tomato, olive oil, salt, and pepper. Let boil until thick. Serve hot; drizzle a little vinegar over each serving.

Lentil soup and legume salad ▶

BAKED BEANS WITH SPICY SAUSAGE
(Koukia ston fourno me pikantika loukanika)

Ingredients

Yield: 6 servings

2 cups small broad beans
1 1/2 cups olive oil
1 cup pork sausage, sliced
1 onion, finely chopped
3 cloves garlic, finely chopped
2 large tomatoes, cubed
1 tsp. oregano
1/2 tsp. sugar
salt
pepper

Preparation
1. Soak beans in cold water for 24 hours. Trim black edge. Boil for 30 minutes in ample water. Drain.
2. Place beans in oven-proof dish. Add tomatoes, onion, garlic, sausage, pinch of salt, sugar, pepper, oregano. Mix well. Add olive oil and one cup water.
3. Bake at 180°C for 45-50 minutes, depending on quality of beans.
4. Serve hot or at room temperature.

BROAD BEAN SALAD
(Koukia ksera salata)

Ingredients

Yield: 8 servings

1 kilo dried broad beans
300 grams olive oil
1 onion
parsley
salt

Preparation
1. Soak beans overnight.
2. The next day, remove skin from beans. Boil in one cup olive oil, 2 cups water, salt, and whole onion.
3. When beans are tender, transfer to blender. Puree beans; add remaining olive oil. Return pureed beans to pot and cook over low heat until thick (puree should have the consistency of mashed potatoes).
4. Transfer to serving platter. Place in refrigerator and chill. Separate into servings, placing each one on a small dish or salad bowl. Garnish with minced onion and minced parsley.

PASTA - RICE

MACARONI PIE
(Makaronopitta)

Ingredients
                            Yield: 6 servings

5 sheets filo
1/4 kilo feta, crumbled
1/2 kilo kefalograviera (or any hard
    cheese), grated
250 grams butter, softened
1 package short macaroni
1 1/2 cups milk
5 eggs

Preparation
1. Boil macaroni in very lightly salted
   water. Strain.
2. In bowl, beat eggs with milk, butter,
   and cheeses. Stir thoroughly.
   Combine with macaroni.
3. Lightly butter bottom of baking pan.
   Line bottom with one sheet of filo;
   brush surface with butter. Repeat
   twice so that pan is lined with three
   sheets of filo. Turn macaroni mix
   into baking dish. Cover with
   remaining sheets of filo, brushing
   each one lightly with butter.
4. Bake at 180°C for about 30 minutes.
   Serve hot.

"PASTITSIO" PIE
(Pastitsio tilihto me filo)

Ingredients
                            Yield: 8 servings

650 grams Greek macaroni (thick,
    hollow spaghetti)
1 1/2 cups grated cheese
150 grams butter
12 sheets filo
nutmeg
salt
pepper

• *For the béchamel sauce:*
300 grams milk
3 eggs
3 Tbs. flour
2 Tbs. butter

Preparation
1. Boil pasta in ample, salted water.
   Strain and return to pot; toss with a
   little melted butter.
2. Meantime, prepare béchamel. (See
   sauce recipes.)
3. Add béchamel to pasta; toss until
   evenly distributed.
4. Lightly grease a baking dish with
   butter. Line bottom with one sheet
   of filo. Brush surface with melted
   butter. Repeat with three more filo
   sheets. Pour half the pasta mixture
   over filo. Cover with four more
   sheets filo, brushing each one with
   butter. Add remaining pasta
   mixture to baking dish and cover
   with remaining filo.
5. Using a sharp knife, cut top filo
   sheet into squares. (Do not pierce
   down to filling.) Bake in preheated
   oven at 180°C for about 40 minutes.

6. Remove from oven. Let cool slightly, cut into squares and serve.

SPAGHETTI WITH YOGURT SAUCE
(Makaronia me yiaourti)

Ingredients

Yield: 6 servings

1/2 kilo spaghetti
3 cups yogurt, strained
2 Tbs. butter, melted
3 cloves garlic
salt – pepper

Preparation
1. Boil pasta in ample salted water. Strain. Toss with half the melted butter.
2. Crush garlic and blend into yogurt. Transfer pasta to serving dish; pour yogurt sauce over pasta. Season with pepper.
3. Toss pasta and sauce; pour remaining butter over top and serve.

▲ *Pasta with garlic and yogurt*

BAKED MACARONI AND EGGPLANT
(Melitzanes me kofto makaronaki sto fourno)

Ingredients

Yield: 8 servings

1/2 kilo short macaroni
1 large eggplant
2 cups feta cheese
3 medium ripe tomatoes, sliced
dash of nutmeg
dried basil
salt
pepper
2-3 Tbs. olive oil

Preparation
1. Cook pasta in salted water until just before the al dente stage. (Pasta will finish cooking in the oven.) Strain, rinse with cold water, return to pot, and toss with olive oil.
2. Cut eggplant into strips about 1 cm thick. Fry in hot oil and drain on kitchen paper.
3. Add eggplant, feta, nutmeg, salt, and pepper to pasta. Stir carefully to avoid crushing pasta and eggplant.
4. Lightly grease an oven-proof dish. Line bottom with tomato slices and sprinkle with basil. Arrange pasta and eggplant mix over tomatoes. Sprinkle a little crumbled feta cheese over the top.
5. Cover with aluminum foil and bake in preheated oven at 180°C for 20 minutes. Remove foil and bake at 200°C for 10 minutes more or until top is browned. Serve hot.

SPAGHETTI AND LOBSTER
(Astakomakaronada)

Ingredients

Yield: 6 servings

1 large lobster (about 1/2 kilo)
300 grams spaghetti
5 Tbs. olive oil
3 large ripe tomatoes, finely chopped
1 large onion, finely chopped
2 spring onions, minced
3 Tbs. parsley, minced
salt
pepper

Preparation
1. Cut lobster open and scoop out flesh. Boil shell, head, and tail in salted water for about 1 hour.
2. Strain lobster, reserving liquid. Transfer lobster water to a clean pot, bring to boil and cook spaghetti.
3. Meantime, brown onion in olive oil. Add tomato and parsley; cook together for about 5 minutes.
4. Cut lobster into small pieces; add to pan with onions and tomatoes. Cook for 3-4 minutes more.
5. Strain spaghetti. Transfer to deep serving dish. Pour lobster sauce over pasta. Serve hot.

GARLIC PASTA
(Skordomakarona)

Ingredients

Yield: 6 servings

1/2 kilo spaghetti
3 Tbs. olive oil
2 large ripe tomatoes,
pressed through grater
2 Tbs. olive oil
2 cloves garlic, crushed
1 medium onion, minced
salt
pepper
dash of sugar

Preparation
1. Prepare tomato sauce: brown onion and garlic in three tablespoons olive oil; add tomato, salt, pepper, and sugar; boil until sauce thickens.
2. Meantime, cook spaghetti in salted water with two tablespoons olive oil. When cooked, strain and toss with remaining olive oil. Serve with tomato sauce.

SPAGHETTI WITH TOMATO SAUCE
(Makaronia me kokkini saltsa)

Ingredients

Yield: 6 servings

1 packet spaghetti
6 Tbs. olive oil
4 large onions, thinly sliced
4 cloves garlic, thinly sliced
3 large ripe tomatoes, pressed through grater
1 glass white wine
cloves
1 cinnamon stick
salt
pepper
butter

Preparation
1. Start sauce by boiling onions and

garlic in a little water until tender and water has evaporated; add olive oil and brown.

2. Add wine to onions; stir to prevent sticking. When tender, add tomatoes, a little water, salt, pepper, cloves, and cinnamon. Simmer until sauce thickens.

3. Meantime, cook pasta in salted water. When done, strain and toss with butter. Serve with sauce.

Rice

CABBAGE AND RICE
(Lahanorizo)

Ingredients

Yield: 6 servings

1 cup rice
1 medium head cabbage
1 onion, finely chopped
1 Tbs. butter
1 Tbs. parsley
1 Tbs. tomato paste
1 lemon
Grated cheese (optional; Greek kefalotiri preferred)
salt
pepper

Preparation

1. Wash cabbage and shred. Brown onion in butter. Add shredded cabbage and sauté with onion.

2. Dilute tomato paste in one cup water and add to cabbage. Stir well.

Add four cups water and bring to boil, then add rice, parsley, and salt.

3. Boil until rice cooked and only scant liquid remains. Serve hot, squeezing a little lemon juice over each serving. Can also be served with grated cheese and freshly ground pepper.

RED RICE
(Tomatorizo)

Ingredients

Yield: 6 servings

2 cups long grain rice
4 large ripe tomatoes, pressed through grater
1/2 cup olive oil
2 cloves garlic, thinly sliced
2 Tbs. parsley, minced
5 cups water
salt
pepper

Preparation

1. Sauté garlic in olive oil. Add tomato and parsley; simmer until water has evaporated and only oil and vegetables are left in pan.

2. Meantime, in separate pot, bring salted water to boil. Add rice and cook until all liquid has been absorbed.

3. When rice is cooked, turn into saucepan with tomato sauce. Stir lightly.

4. Serve hot; sprinkle freshly ground pepper over each serving.

MEAT

PORK AND OLIVES
(Hirino me elyes
ke kokini saltsa)

Ingredients

Yield: 8 servings

2 kilos pork, cut into portions
1/2 kilo large green olives
1 bay leaf
1 jar pickled onions, strained
4 cups tomato juice
1/2 bunch parsley, minced
4 Tbs. butter

Preparation
1. Mix ingredients together in a large bowl. Transfer to clay pot. Bake at 250°C for about one hour. Reduce heat to 150°C and bake for another 60 minutes.
2. Serve with pasta cooked al dente.

PORK WITH QUINCE
(Hirino kidonato)

Ingredients

Yield: 8 servings

1/4 cup olive oil
1 cup finely chopped onions
1 kilo lean pork, cubed
1/2 kilo stewing onions
1 Tbs. cloves
1 cup Mavrodafni wine (or dark, sweet red wine)
1 stick cinnamon

salt
1 1/2 kilos quinces
1 Tbs. sugar

Preparation
1. Heat 4-5 spoonfuls of olive oil in a deep frying pan or shallow saucepan. Sauté onions with pork, browning meat on all sides. Using slotted spoon, remove meat and set aside. Push cloves into stewing onions and add to pan. Sauté.
2. Return pork to pan; add wine, cinnamon, and salt. Bring to boil and simmer over medium heat for about 5 minutes. Add one cup water, cover, and simmer for 30-40 minutes, until meat is not quite cooked through. Add water if necessary.
3. Peel and quarter quinces. Remove seeds and tough center. Cut each piece in half, lengthwise. Sauté onions in remaining oil until brown on all sides.
4. Heat oven to 180°C. Transfer meat, quince, and onions to oven-proof or clay baking dish. Sprinkle half the sugar over quince pieces. Pour sauce over meat and vegetables, then sprinkle with remaining sugar.
5. Cover (with lid or aluminum foil) and bake for 30-40 minutes, until quince is soft and lightly caramelized. While cooking,

▲ *Pork with quince*

frequently baste meat and quince with sauce from pan. Serve hot.

PORK AND CABBAGE
(Hirino me lahano)

Ingredients
                              Yield: 8 servings
1 kilo pork
1 cabbage
juice of one lemon
2 Tbs. butter
salt

Preparation
1. Rinse meat and place in pot to boil. Just before pork is cooked through, add chopped cabbage, butter, and salt. Cook until cabbage is done.
2. Five minutes before removing from heat, add lemon juice.

PORK "LAGOTO"
(Lagoto)

Ingredients
                              Yield: 6 servings
1 kilo pork from shoulder blade, cut into
     small pieces
5-6 cloves garlic, crushed
1 onion, finely chopped
3 slices bread soaked in red wine
1 large tomato, crushed
1 cup olive oil
1 cup walnuts, coarsely chopped
2 Tbs. red wine vinegar
salt
fresh ground pepper

Preparation
1. In non-stick frying pan, brown meat in olive oil for 5 minutes.
2. Remove meat and set aside. To pan, add onion and cook for 3-4 minutes until reddish in color.
3. Empty onions and frying oil into deep cooking pot. Add browned meat, tomato, half cup of water, a little salt and pepper; cover, and let simmer for 20 minutes. Using a slotted spoon, transfer meat to oven-proof dish.
4. With your hand, squeeze wine from bread and add to pot with garlic, salt, vinegar and one cup water. Simmer for 10 minutes, stirring continuously until sauce thickens.
5. Cover meat with sauce and place in preheated oven for 20-25 minutes until golden brown crust forms.
6. Serve hot with a robust red wine.

PORK WITH LEEKS AND PRUNES
(Hirino me prassa ke damaskina)

Ingredients

Yield: 6 servings

1 kilo pork shoulder-blade, cubed
1 kilo leeks, sliced
1/2 cup celery, finely chopped
8 dried prunes, pitted and halved
1 small onion, finely chopped
1 Tbs. tomato paste
3/4 cup olive oil
salt
freshly ground pepper

Preparation
1. Lightly sauté onion in olive oil for 2-3 minutes without browning. Add pork; brown meat on all sides. Add 1 cup water, pinch of salt. Simmer for approximately 30 minutes.
2. Remove meat and set aside. Add leeks to saucepan, stir in 2 cups water and pinch of salt. Cook over medium heat for 25 minutes.
3. Return meat to pot. Dilute tomato paste in half cup water and add to meat and leeks, along with prunes and celery. Stir and cook for 20 minutes more until all water has been absorbed.
4. Serve hot. Season with freshly ground pepper.

LEMON PORK
(Hirino Lemonato)

Ingredients

Yield: 6 servings

1 1/2 kilos pork shoulder-blade, cut into portions
1 large onion, finely chopped
1 cup celery
2 carrots, finely chopped
2 large potatoes, quartered
juice of one large lemon
3/4 cup olive oil
salt
pepper

Preparation
1. Lightly brown onion in olive oil. Add meat and brown on all sides. Add 1 1/2 cups water, cover, and let simmer for 25 minutes.
2. Add potatoes, celery, carrot, salt, pepper, and 2 1/2 cups water. Cover and cook for 30 minutes more. Add lemon juice and serve.

ROAST SUCKLING PIG
(Gourounopoulo Psito)

Ingredients
Yield: 10 servings
1 whole suckling pig, about 8-10 kilos in
weight
1 1/2 cups olive oil
juice of 3 large lemons
1 Tbs. salt
1/2 Tbs. ground pepper
1 Tbs. oregano
2 cloves garlic, crushed

Preparation
1. Combine olive oil, lemon juice, garlic, and seasonings. Baste pig, inside and out, with sauce.
2. Place pig in a large baking pan, stomach-side up. Cook at 180°C for one hour. Increase heat to 200°C, then turn pig over to brown on other side. Cook for another 60 minutes.
3. When meat is done, turn oven to grill setting. Brown suckling pig on all sides, turning as necessary.

RABBIT WITH THYME
(Lagos i kouneli me thymari)

Ingredients
Yield: 8 servings
1 large rabbit or hare, whole
4-5 sprigs thyme, preferably whole
flowered branches
1 cup white wine
1/2 tsp. pepper
2-3 small onions, whole
1/2 tsp. cumin
1/2 tsp. sugar
2 Tbs. vinegar
2-3 cloves
3 Tbs. olive oil
salt

Preparation
1. Rinse rabbit under cold running water. Place in large bowl. Rub all over, including inside, with salt, pepper, cumin, and sugar. Push cloves into onions, and place onions in rabbit's belly.
2. Line bottom of Dutch oven with thyme branches. Place rabbit on branches. Pour olive oil, wine, and vinegar over meat. Cover and bake at 180°C for 3-4 hours. Do not open lid while cooking. Serve rabbit in its sauce, with a large green salad as an accompaniment.

RABBIT WITH OLIVES AND CAPERS
(Kouneli me prassines elyes ke kapari)

Ingredients

Yield: 8 servings

1 large rabbit, cut in pieces
1 Tbs. fine capers
20 green Halkidiki olives
3/4 cup olive oil
1 small onion, grated
2 spring onions, finely chopped
1 cup lukewarm dry white wine
1 tsp. honey
1/2 cup warm white wine vinegar
salt
coarsely ground green pepper

Preparation

1. Heat olive oil in saucepan and sauté onion for 3-4 minutes but do not brown. Add rabbit and brown on all sides. Add 1 1/2 cups water, cover, and simmer for about 20 minutes.
2. Rinse brine from capers and olives. Add to pot. Stir to distribute evenly, add 1 cup water, and cook for another 20 minutes.
3. In separate bowl, dilute honey with wine and vinegar. When meat is done, add honey-wine sauce to pot. Serve in sauce, with boiled potatoes on the side.

STUFFED RABBIT
(Kouneli yemisto)

Ingredients

Yield: 8 servings

1 medium rabbit
1 lamb's liver (not very large)
1 cup pine nuts
2 cups dry white wine
1 cup rice
3 Tbs. dill, minced
2 medium onions, finely chopped
1/2 cup raisins
3/4 cup olive oil
2 bay leaves
pinch of thyme
salt
pepper

Preparation

1. Clean and gut rabbit. Prepare stuffing: brown onions in a small amount of olive oil. When deep golden in color, add finely chopped liver and stir. Cook until all liquid has been absorbed and liver is browned on all sides.
2. Add wine and stir. Add dill, season with salt and pepper. Add little water and bring to boil. Simmer for 10 minutes. Add rice, pine nuts, 3 cups water, and let simmer.
3. Five minutes before removing from heat, stir in raisins. Correct seasoning, then remove from heat, and set aside to cool. Rub rabbit with salt and pepper, inside and out. Spoon stuffing into rabbit cavity.
4. Truss rabbit, making sure to sew

stomach securely so stuffing does not fall out. Season rabbit; pour sauce made from one cup wine, olive oil and thyme over meat.

5. Arrange bay leaves on bottom of Dutch oven. Place rabbit on top and cover with lid.

6. Preheat oven to 200°C. Cook rabbit at medium temperature for about 2 hours. Ten minutes before ready, remove lid so rabbit can brown lightly. Cut string, remove stuffing and serve.

GOAT WITH OREGANO AND OLIVE OIL
(Katsiki ladorigani)

Ingredients

Yield: 6 servings

1 cup virgin olive oil
leg of goat (1 1/2 kilos in weight)
1 cup dry white wine
1 Tbs. oregano
1 Tbs. flour
1 tsp. salt
pepper
juice of one large lemon

Preparation

1. Cut meat into small pieces and wash. Place in pot without draining. Cover and simmer until all the water has evaporated.

2. Add olive oil and stir until meat lightly browned. Add wine. Dilute flour with 1 1/2 cups water and add to pot with oregano,

salt, pepper, and lemon juice. Cover and simmer for 30-35 minutes.

3. Serve in its sauce, with fried potatoes as an accompaniment.

GOAT WITH FRESH GRAPE LEAVES
(Katsiki me freska filla ambelou)

Ingredients

Yield: 6 servings
1 1/2 kilo goat (shoulder blade or leg), cut in bite-sized pieces
1 1/2 kilo tender grapevine leaves
bunch of grapevine roots
5 spring onions, finely chopped
1 Tbs. dill, finely chopped
3/4 cup olive oil
salt
black pepper

Preparation

1. Sauté onions in olive oil for 2-3 minutes. Add goat meat and brown on all sides. Add one cup water, cover, and simmer for 20 minutes.

2. Cut large vine leaves in half. Wash leaves, roots, and dill. Combine and add seasonings. Put in pot with goat and, if necessary, add a little water. Cover and boil over low heat for 40-50 minutes. Serve hot.

STUFFED LAMB SHOULDER-BLADE
(Spalla arniou yemisti)

Ingredients

Yield: 6 servings

1 shoulder-blade of lamb, between 1 1/2
    and 2 kilos in weight
1/2 cup olive oil
1 tsp. butter
2 spring onions, finely chopped
1 sprig dill, minced
1/2 kilo ground beef
3/4 cup rice
2 cups beef broth
pinch of cinnamon
salt
pepper
1 Tbs. flour
juice of one large lemon

Preparation

1. In saucepan, sauté onions in olive
   oil and butter. Add ground beef and
   dill. Cook, while stirring
   continuously so meat does not stick.
   Add rice and broth. Stir and let
   summer until liquid has been
   absorbed. Add seasonings and salt;
   let cool.
2. Rinse lamb shoulder-blade. (Ask
   butcher to cut slit in meat so you
   can stuff it.) Rub meat with salt and
   pepper; spoon rice and ground beef
   stuffing into split.
3. Arrange shoulder-blade on vine
   branches or grill. Baste with lemon
   and olive oil, the dredge with flour
   to form crisp skin. Cook at 180°C
   for about one hour.

BAKED GOAT WITH TOMATOES
(Katsiki me tomates sto fourno)

Ingredients

Yield: 8 servings

2 kilos goat, cut into large portion
1 kilo ripe tomatoes, sliced
1 cup olive oil
salt
pepper

Preparation

1. Boil goat meat in ample salted water
   over high heat for about 30 minutes.
   Using slotted spoon, remove and
   arrange in large baking dish. Season
   with salt and pepper, then cover
   with tomato slices. Add two cups of
   broth from goat; pour olive oil over
   tomatoes and season with salt and
   pcpper.
2. Bake at 180°C for about 2 hours.
   Before removing from oven, make
   sure meat is cooked through. Serve
   hot in its sauce.

LAMB WITH FENNEL
(Arni me finokio)

Ingredients

Yield: 6 servings

1 kilo spring lamb
2 fennel bulbs
1 large onion, finely chopped
3/4 cups olive oil
juice of one large lemon
1 tsp. flour
salt
pepper

Preparation

1. Rinse meat and cut into small pieces. In large saucepan, heat olive oil and lightly brown onion. Add meat, stir with fork to brown on all sides. Add one cup water, cover, and simmer for about 20 minutes.
2. Clean fennel, cut into small pieces, and add to pot. Add one more cup water, season with salt and pepper, stir, and cover; let cook for 45 minutes more.
3. Dissolve flour in lemon juice. Add to saucepan, shaking gently to evenly distribute juices. Let rest for 10 minutes before serving.

LAMB WITH PRUNES
(Arni me damaskina)

Ingredients

Yield: 6 servings

1 1/2 kilos lamb, cut into portions
700 grams prunes, pitted
2 Tbs. butter
1 Tbs. flour
3 Tbs. sugar
juice of 2 lemons
1 onion, finely chopped
salt
pepper

Preparation

1. Rinse meat and let drain. Season with salt and pepper; pour half the lemon juice over meat, sprinkle with chopped onion and let marinade for about one hour.
2. In saucepan, heat butter; brown meat. Remove meat from pan, add flour, and stir vigorously with wooden spoon to form a smooth roux. Stir in marinade; add meat and let simmer over low heat.
3. Add prunes. Cover and let cook through.
4. Before removing from heat, add sugar and remaining lemon juice. Serve with rice or fried potatoes.

LAMB STEW
(Arni kapama)

Ingredients

Yield: 8 servings

1 1/2 kilos young lamb, cut in
   portions
1 1/2 Tbs. butter
1 cup red wine
1 Tbs. flour
1 large onion
1 ripe tomato, cubed
1 stalk celery
1 carrot, sliced
4 cloves
1 stick cinnamon
salt
pepper

Preparation

1. Rinse meat under cold running water; drain in colander. Place butter in large, heavy-bottom saucepan and heat until it begins to foam. Add meat and brown on all sides. Remove meat and set aside.
2. To hot butter, add flour and stir roux for 2-3 minutes. Add wine, stir. Add tomato and one cup water. Simmer sauce for 10-15 minutes. Strain in fine sieve.
3. Return sauce to pot. Push cloves into onion. Add to sauce along with meat, carrot, celery, cinnamon stick, salt, and pepper. Add a little water and simmer for 50 minutes. Serve hot.

BAKED LAMB WITH ARTICHOKES AND YOGURT
(Arni me agginares ke yiaourti sto fourno)

Ingredients

Yield: 8 servings

1 1/2 kilos lamb, preferably whole
   shoulder-blade or leg
2 kilos artichokes
1/2 kilo thick yogurt
3 eggs
1 cup olive oil
1 large lemon
1 tsp. salt
1/2 tsp. nutmeg
1/2 tsp. pepper

Preparation

1. Clean artichokes and rub with lemon to prevent discoloring. Boil in plenty of water for 5 minutes.
2. Season meat with salt and pepper. Place in baking pan. Add olive oil and 1 cup water. Bake at 180°C for 55 minutes.
3. Beat yogurt, eggs, and nutmeg together. Place artichokes around lamb. Pour yogurt sauce over meat and vegetables. Continue baking at 180°C for 25 minutes more or until yogurt topping is brown.
4. Serve hot or at room temperature.

LAMB FRICASSEE
(Arni fricassee me maroulia)

Ingredients
                    Yield: 6 servings
1 kilo lamb, cut in small pieces
2 large heads of lettuce, coarsely chopped
1 medium onion, grated
6-7 spring onions, finely chopped
1 bunch dill, finely chopped
3/4 cup olive oil
2 eggs
juice from 2 medium-sized lemons
salt
pepper

Preparation
1. Sauté grated onion in olive oil until lightly browned. Add lamb and brown on all sides.
2. Add green onions and 3 cups water. Cover and simmer for 30 minutes.
3. When meat almost cooked, add dill, salt, pepper, and lettuce. Turn up heat and cook for 15 minutes more.
4. Beat eggs with wire whisk until foamy. While still beating, gradually add a little lemon juice, then a little broth from pot. Continue until all the lemon juice has been whisked into the eggs.
5. Pour egg-lemon-broth sauce into pot and shake to distribute evenly. Turn off heat but leave pot on stove for a final boil.
6. Serve hot in its sauce.

STUFFED LEG OF LAMB
(Bouti arniou yemisto me kefalotiri)

Ingredients
                    Yield: 6 servings
1 leg of lamb (about 1 1/2 kilos in weight)
200 grams ground beef or goat
2 Tbs. mint, minced
40 grams grated kefalotiri (or other hard cheese)
3 eggs
4 Tbs. olive oil
2 medium cloves garlic
salt
pepper

Preparation
1. In mixing bowl, combine ground meat, cheese, eggs, mint, salt, and pepper.
2. Remove bone from leg of lamb and pound meat to loosen flesh. Spoon meat and egg mix into center. Truss with kitchen thread. Rub skin with garlic and wrap entire leg in non-stick cooking paper drizzled with olive oil.
3. Preheat oven to 200°C. Place lamb in Dutch oven. Pour remaining olive oil around lamb, cover, and cook at 180°C for about 2 hours.
4. Twenty minutes before meat is done, remove lid and non-stick paper. Pour wine around meat. Remove from oven, then let rest for 10-15 minutes before serving; slice while hot.

LAMB WITH ZUCCHINI
(Arni me kolokithakia)

Ingredients

Yield: 6 servings

3 cups olive oil for frying
10 small zucchinis (courgettes)
2 cloves garlic, minced
2 ripe tomatoes, cubed
2 large potatoes cut into large pieces for frying
1 1/2 kilo lamb, cut into portions
1 large onion, grated
1/2 tsp. sugar
salt
pepper

Preparation

1. Wash zucchini. Slit lengthwise on one side; slip a piece of garlic into cut.
2. In frying pan, heat one cup olive oil and lightly fry zucchini for 7-8 minutes until brown on all sides. Drain on kitchen paper. Add one more cup olive oil to pan and fry potatoes. When cooked, drain on kitchen paper.
3. In heavy-bottomed saucepan, heat one cup olive oil. Brown onion for 3-4 minutes. Add meat and brown. Add two cups water, cover, and let simmer for 30 minutes.
4. Check meat with fork to see if cooked through. Meantime, in separate bowl, stir salt, pepper, and sugar into cubed tomatoes. When meat is done, push meat apart to make room in bottom of saucepan for zucchini and potatoes. Pour tomato sauce over meat and vegetables, cover, and simmer for 20-25 minutes.
5. Remove cover, turn off heat, but leave pot on stove for one last simmer. Serve hot or at room temperature.

"KLEFTIKO"
(Arnaki kleftiko)

Ingredients

Yield: 6 servings

1 kilo boneless lamb, cut into portions
2 Tbs. lemon juice
200 grams kefalotiri, thinly sliced
1/3 cup olive oil
oregano
minced parsley
salt
pepper

▲ *"Kleftiko" lamb*

Preparation

1. Place meat in mixing bowl. Add olive oil, oregano, parsley, salt, and pepper.
2. Toss ingredients together until meat is coated. Add lemon juice, toss again.
3. Cut non-stick kitchen paper into strips large enough to wrap twice around each piece of meat.
4. Arrange meat on paper. Place one slice of cheese on meat and wrap shut. Seal ends of each packet to prevent juices from escaping.
5. Place packets next to one another in baking dish (cheese side up). Bake at 200°C for one hour.

SPAGHETTI WITH LAMB SAUCE
(Makaronia me saltsa apo kokkinisto arni)

Ingredients

Yield: 6 servings

1 kilo lamb (shoulder-blade or ribs), cut into portions
2 medium onions, thinly sliced
2 Tbs. parsley, minced
2 medium ripe tomatoes, finely chopped
1/3 cup olive oil
3/4 cup unresinated white wine
1 packet long macaroni (No. 7 or No. 10)
2 Tbs. butter
salt
pepper

Preparation

1. Rinse meat and let drain. Pour oil into deep, non-stick saucepan. Add meat and brown lightly over low heat.
2. Add onions and brown. Add wine, cover, and simmer for 15 minutes. Add parsley, tomato, salt, pepper, and one cup water. Cover and simmer over low heat for 45 minutes.
3. In separate saucepan, bring salted water to boil. Cook pasta in water; when done, strain and toss with butter.
4. Serve pasta in shallow dishes. Top with lamb and sauce.

SKEWERED LAMB
(Souvlakia arnissia)

Ingredients

Yield: 6 servings

1 kilo lamb (shoulder or leg)
6 Tbs. olive oil
juice of 1 lemon
salt
pepper
1 bell pepper, cut into pieces
4-5 cherry tomatoes
oregano

Preparation

1. Cut lamb into large cubes (roughly 2.5 cms thick). Push cubes onto skewers.
2. In shallow bowl, beat together the olive oil, lemon juice, salt, pepper, and oregano. Marinade lamb kebobs in sauce for one hour,

turning occasionally so all sides are coated.
3. Cook over barbecue or under electric grill.

Bell peppers and tomatoes can be skewered between meat cubes.

SPICY BEEF WITH THASSOS OLIVES
(Pikantiko kokkinisto moschari me elyes Thassou)

Ingredients

Yield: 8 servings

1 kilo lean beef (rump)
4 large ripe tomatoes, pressed through grater
2 large onions, finely chopped
1/2 cup brandy
2 cloves garlic, minced
1 cup olive oil
1 1/2 Tbs. parsley, minced
1 bay leaf
1 tsp. oregano
1 1/2 cups black olives
1/2 tsp. grated lemon or orange peel
salt
pepper

Preparation
1. Soak olives in fresh water for two hours to rinse brine and swell. Change water 7-8 times, then drain olives on kitchen paper. With sharp knife, slice open and remove pit.
2. Using a very sharp knife, cut slits into meat. Push olives, garlic, and parsley into slits.
3. In a large, heavy-bottomed saucepan, heat olive oil. Add meat and brown on all sides. Add onions, season with salt; pour in brandy.
4. Add tomatoes, a little parsley, oregano, bay leaf, and two cups water. Cover and simmer over very low heat for about two hours. Occasionally check meat and correct seasoning or add water, if necessary.
5. When meat is done and sauce has thickened, remove lid and let cook for a few minutes uncovered. Sprinkle with grated lemon or orange peel and let cool slightly before serving.

BEEF WITH CHICKPEAS
(Moschari me revithia)

Ingredients
Yield: 8 servings
1/2 kilo chickpeas (garbanzo beans)
1 kilo beef, from side
1 cup olive oil
2 medium onions, finely chopped
2 medium tomatoes, crushed
1 bay leaf
salt
pepper

Preparation
1. Soak chickpeas in cold water for eight hours. Strain and boil in plenty of salted water for 10 minutes. Strain, rinse, and rub lightly to loosen and remove skin.
2. Lightly brown onions in olive oil. Add meat, turning with fork to brown on all sides.
3. Add 3 cups water and bring to boil. With slotted spoon, remove foam. Cover and let simmer for 45-50 minutes until tender and almost cooked. Add chickpeas, bay leaf, salt, and pepper. If stew looks too dry, add 1 or 1 1/2 cups water and cook for 30-40 minutes more.
4. Serve hot in its sauce. Sauce should be thick and rich.

"SOFRITO"
(Sofrito Kerkiraiko)

Ingredients
Yield: 8 servings
1 kilo boneless beef
1 bunch parsley, finely chopped
6 cloves garlic, thinly sliced
1 Tbs. butter
2 Tbs. olive oil
1 cup white vinegar
2 cups flour
salt
1 tsp. freshly ground pepper

Preparation
1. Rinse meat and drain on kitchen towels.
2. In small dish, mix salt and pepper; place flour in separate, larger dish. One at a time, roll meat cubes first in salt-and-pepper mix and then in flour.
3. Gently shake excess flour off meat. Heat olive oil and butter in frying pan and cook meat until lightly browned.
4. Arrange half of browned beef in the bottom of a large, heavy-bottomed saucepan. Sprinkle generously with parsley and half the garlic. Layer remaining beef over top, and sprinkle with parsley and remaining garlic. Add vinegar and one cup lukewarm water. Cover and simmer for at least 50-60 minutes. Meat must be very tender and sauce thick.

BEEF IN WINE
(*Moschari krassato*)

Ingredients

Yield: 8 servings

1 1/2 kilos beef (bottom round roast)
4 Tbs. olive oil
1 onion, crushed
1 cup red wine
salt
pepper
cumin

Preparation

1. Rinse meat and drain on kitchen paper. Season with salt and pepper.
2. In saucepan, heat butter until bubbly. Add meat and brown on all sides. Add onion and wine; season with salt, pepper, and cumin. Cover and simmer over low heat for about two hours. Check occasionally, adding enough water to keep meat from sticking. When cooked through and deep golden brown, remove from heat. Slice thinly, then let simmer in sauce for about 10 minutes.

RICE WITH THREE MEATS
(*Pilafi me tria kreata*)

Ingredients

Yield: 10 servings

1/2 kilo beef
1/2 kilo goat or lamb
1/2 chicken
3 cups rice
2 Tbs. butter
salt – pepper

Preparation

1. Boil meat together in a large pot of salted water until cooked through.
2. Using slotted spoon, remove meat from pot. Strain broth. Return 10 cups of broth to pot and bring to boil. Add rice, stir, and simmer for about 20 minutes.
3. Return meat to pot and cook with rice for 10 minutes more. Remove from heat. Heat butter until melted. Pour over rice, and cover with a cotton towel. Let stand for 10 minutes; serve immediately with freshly ground pepper.

MEATBALLS
(*Keftedes*)

Ingredients

Yield: 10 servings

1/2 kilo ground beef
1/2 kilo ground lamb
4 cloves garlic, crushed
2 cups crustless bread soaked in a little red wine
2 Tbs. dry breadcrumbs
2 Tbs. fresh parsley, minced
1 egg
1 tsp. oregano
2 Tbs. olive oil
olive oil for frying
salt – pepper
cumin

Preparation

1. In mixing bowl, combine ground

beef with ground lamb. Add breadcrumbs, drained bread, egg, garlic, parsley, oregano, olive oil, salt, cumin, and pepper.

2. Knead ingredients together until thoroughly combined. Roll piece of meat mix in the palm of your hand, then slam into bowl. Repeat with remaining meat.

3. Knead mixture together, then let rest for 15 minutes.

4. Shape meat mix into balls, then fry in olive oil. Serve hot or at room temperature.

SAUCY MEATBALLS
(Keftedes me saltsa)

Ingredients

Yield: 10 servings

1 kilo ground beef
1/2 tsp. oregano
1/2 tsp. nutmeg
1/2 tsp. thyme
1/2 tsp. cumin
1 clove garlic, crushed
1 Tbs. parsley, minced
4-5 Tbs. dry breadcrumbs
1 egg
1 large onion, finely chopped
2 large tomatoes, finely chopped (or 3 Tbs. tomato sauce)
1/2 cup olive oil
salt
pepper

Preparation
In mixing bowl, combine ground beef with spices, garlic,

breadcrumbs, egg, and onion. Meantime, in a small saucepan bring tomato (or tomato sauce) and 2 cups water to boil, then simmer for 10 minutes. Add olive oil. Shape meat into small meatballs and drop into sauce. Simmer for 15-20 minutes or until sauce is thick.

MEATBALLS WITH LEEKS
(Keftedes me prassa)

Ingredients

Yield: 8 servings

1 kilo leeks
1 bunch leaf celery, finely chopped
1/2 cup olive oil
4 large ripe tomatoes, pressed through grater
salt
pepper

• For the meatballs:
1 kilo ground meat
200 grams bread
1 egg
1 small glass white wine
3 Tbs. milk
1 large onion, minced
3 Tbs. olive oil
dash of cumin
salt
pepper

Preparation
1. Wash leeks and celery; chop coarsely. Place in saucepan with tomatoes, salt, pepper, and enough water to prevent

sticking and let cook slowly.

2. Meantime, prepare meatballs by combining all ingredients. Shape into walnut-sized balls.

3. When leeks half cooked, arrange meatballs over vegetables. Pour olive oil over leeks. When meat cooked on one side, turn and let cook on the other. Serve hot.

MEATBALLS WITH MASTIC AND OUZO
(Keftedakia me mastiha ke ouzo)

Ingredients

Yield: 6 servings

250 grams ground beef
250 grams ground pork
2 eggs
2 barley rusks
1 medium onion, grated
2 Tbs. ouzo
1 piece mastic, crushed
1 Tbs. vinegar
20 small cubes feta cheese
2 Tbs. flour
1 cup olive oil for frying
salt
pepper

Preparation

1. Soak rusks in cold water to soften. Squeeze out water and place in large bowl.

2. Add meat, eggs, onion, ouzo, mastic crushed in a little flour, vinegar, salt, and pepper. Knead together and let

stand for at least two hours for flavors to emerge.

3. Shape mixture into small balls. Poke ball and push a feta cube into indentation. Reshape slightly so that cheese is covered.

4. Roll balls in flour then fry in hot olive oil. Serve hot or at room temperature.

BEEF PATTIES WITH CHEESE
(Biftekia me tiri)

Ingredients

Yield: 8 servings

1 kilo ground beef
150 grams gruyere cheese, finely chopped
3 Tbs. olive oil
2 eggs
2-3 onions, finely chopped
1 clove garlic, crushed
minced parsley
oregano
250 grams crustless bread, soaked (squeeze out liquid before using)
salt
pepper

Preparation

1. Sauté onion in olive oil until tender.

2. In mixing bowl, combine sautéed onion, meat, cheese, garlic, lightly beaten eggs, parsley, oregano, bread, salt, and pepper. Knead until thoroughly blended.

3. Shape meat into beef patties; cook under grill. Serve with fried potatoes and a green salad.

SMYRNA BALLS WITH OLIVES
(*Soutzoukakia Smirneika me elyes*)

Ingredients

Yield: 6 servings

1/2 kilo ground beef
1/2 kilo ground lamb
2 cloves garlic, crushed
1 cup dry breadcrumbs
1/2 tsp. cumin
4 Tbs. red wine
1 tsp. salt
1 tsp. pepper
3 Tbs. olive oil

• *For the sauce*
2 large tomatoes, peeled and
  crushed
1 tsp. tomato paste diluted in one cup
  water

2 Tbs. olive oil
1/2 tsp. salt
1 cup green olives

Preparation
1. In mixing bowl, combine meat, breadcrumbs, wine, garlic, salt, and pepper.
2. Knead ingredients together until thoroughly combined. Shape into small sausages and set on kitchen paper while preparing sauce.
3. Place sauce ingredients in saucepan. Bring to boil and let simmer.
4. When sauce starts to thicken, carefully place meatballs in sauce. Add olives. Simmer for 8-10 minutes.
5. Serve hot with rice or fried potatoes.

▲ *Smyrna balls with olives*

"PASTITSIO"
(Pastitsio)

Ingredients

Yield: 8 servings

1 kilo ground beef
1 onion, finely chopped
1/2 cup olive oil
3 large ripe tomatoes, pressed through
  grater
1 demitasse white wine
1/2 bunch parsley, minced
2 cups grated cheese (kasseri, gruyere,
  or kefalotiri)
1/2 kilo Greek macaroni (long, hollow
  spaghetti)
2 Tbs. butter
1 egg
dry breadcrumbs
grated cinnamon (optional)
Béchamel sauce (see sauce recipes)
salt
pepper
nutmeg

Preparation
1. In deep frying pan, brown onions and ground meat. Add wine. Stir in parsley, cinnamon, tomatoes, salt, and pepper. Let simmer until liquid has been absorbed. Remove from heat; stir in half the grated cheese and 1/2 cup dried breadcrumbs.
2. Cook pasta in salted water until only slightly tender. Strain, toss with melted butter. Stir in lightly beaten eggs and remaining cheese.
3. Lightly butter a baking dish and sprinkle with dried breadcrumbs. Arrange half the pasta in bottom of pan. Pour meat mix over pasta. Arrange remaining pasta over meat.
4. Pour béchamel sauce over pasta. Sprinkle with grated cheese and breadcrumbs, then drizzle butter over top. Bake at 180°C for about one hour. Remove, cut when lukewarm and serve.

"MOUSSAKA"
(Moussakas)

Ingredients

Yield: 8 servings

1 kilo ground beef and pork (or beet and
  lamb)
1 kilo potatoes
1 1/2 kilos eggplant or zucchini
1 cup grated cheese
1 Tbs. butter
1 onion
4 large ripe tomatoes
olive oil for frying
salt
pepper
cumin
dash of ground cinnamon
dry breadcrumbs

Preparation
1. In deep saucepan, brown meat and onion in olive oil. Stir in cinnamon, tomato, salt, cumin, and pepper; let simmer over low heat until liquid has been absorbed. Remove from heat. Add 1/3 cheese and 3-4 tablespoons breadcrumbs. Stir well.
2. Clean potatoes and trim eggplants.

Cut into thin slices (about 1 cm thick) and fry. Drain on kitchen paper.

3. Lightly butter large baking dish; sprinkle with breadcrumbs.

4. Layer potatoes on bottom of pan; sprinkle with a little grated cheese. Spread meat mixture over potatoes. Layer eggplant slices over meat. Pour béchamel sauce over eggplant. Sprinkle with a little grated cheese and breadcrumbs, then drizzle with melted butter. Bake moussaka at 180°C for about one hour. Let cool for 15-20 minutes, then cut into squares and serve.

BEEF OR CHICKEN "YIOUVETSI"
(Yiouvetsi fournou me moschari, kotopoulo i hirino)

Ingredients
Yield: 8-10 servings
1 1/2 kilo beef (shoulder-blade) or pork or1 whole chicken
2 large ripe tomatoes, sliced 1-2 cms thick
1 packet kritharaki (barley shaped pasta)
1 medium onion, quartered
1 Tbs. olive oil
1 Tbs. butter
salt
pepper
grated cheese

Preparation

1. Rinse meat under cold, running water and cut into large pieces. Place in lidded clay pot. Pour olive oil and two cups water over meat and arrange sliced tomatoes over top. Cover and bake in center of oven at 200°C for 45-50 minutes. Lower heat to 180°C and cook for one hour more.

2. When meat is cooked, boil pasta with onion for 5 minutes. Drain and add butter. Stir well so that pasta is coated. Season lightly with salt and pepper.

3. Open pot and pour pasta around meat. Lightly season meat with salt and pepper. Cover and return to oven. Bake at 200°C for 8 minutes. Turn off heat and let pot stand in hot oven for 20 minutes. Add grated cheese before serving.

"Yiouvetsi" ▶

CHICKEN WITH OKRA
(Kotopoulo me bamyes)

Ingredients
Yield: 8-10 servings
1 chicken, cut into portions
1 cup olive oil
1 kilo fresh okra
1 large onion, sliced
2 large ripe tomatoes, crushed
2 large tomatoes, sliced
juice of one large lemon
salt
pepper
cumin

Preparation
1. Top and tail okra; if very large cut in half. Clean and let stand in colander until thoroughly drained. Place in baking dish and salt. Add lemon juice. Clean chicken and season with salt, pepper, and cumin.
2. Drain okra and combine with crushed tomatoes; season with salt and pepper.
3. Place chicken in baking dish. Cover with okra and tomato mix, spreading evenly over poultry. Pour over olive oil and arrange tomato and onion slices on top. Cover with aluminum foil and bake at 180°C for 30 minutes. Remove foil and bake for 25 minutes more.

CAPON "PASTITSADA"
(Kokoras pastitsada)

Ingredients
Yield: 8 servings
1 capon, about 4-5 kilos, cut into pieces
1/2 cup olive oil
7 white onions, finely chopped
3 Tbs. tomato paste
2 cinnamon sticks
5 cloves
1 tsp. freshly ground black pepper
1/2 tsp. nutmeg
1/2 tsp. dried basil
1 package long, hollow macaroni
grated cheese

Preparation
1. Sauté onions in olive oil over medium heat until lightly browned. Add seasonings. Stir for 2-3 minutes, then add poultry. Cook for 4-5 minutes until brown.
2. Add 2 cups water and let simmer for approximately 15 minutes. Dilute tomato paste in one cup of water and add to pot. Cover and let simmer for at least 55-60 minutes until sauce is thick.
3. In separate pot, boil pasta, drain and set aside. Remove poultry from pot and set aside. Add pasta top sauce and stir until completely coated.
4. Serve pasta hot with sauce and meat. Top with grated cheese.

ROAST OREGANO CHICKEN WITH POTATOES
(Kotopoulo ston fourno me patates ke rigani)

Ingredients

Yield: 8 servings

1 chicken, halved or cut into portions
2 kilos medium potatoes, quartered
1 1/2 cups olive oil
juice of 4 lemons
oregano
salt
pepper

Preparation

1. Rinse chicken and place in baking pan.
2. Pour half lemon juice over chicken. Sprinkle with oregano; season with salt and pepper. Arrange potatoes around chicken. Pour remaining lemon juice over potatoes. Sprinkle with more oregano, then season with salt and pepper. Using your fingers, toss lightly to make sure potatoes are coated.

▼ *Roast chicken with potatoes*

3. Pour olive oil and one cup water over pan. Cook for 1 1/2 hours at 180°C. Serve hot.

CAPON STUFFED WITH GROUND MEAT AND PINE NUTS
(Kokoras yemistos me kima ke koukounaria)

Ingredients

Yield: 8 servings

1 capon, approximately 3 kilos
*   in weight*
3 cups ground lamb
2 Tbs. pine nuts
1 large onion, finely chopped
2 Tbs. dried breadcrumbs
1 1/2 cups dry white wine
1 large ripe tomato, peeled and
*   crushed*
3 Tbs. butter
1 Tbs. parsley, finely chopped
3 cups chicken broth
1/2 tsp. ground cinnamon
salt
pepper

Preparation

1. Split poultry. Remove innards, clean, mince, and set aside. Rinse capon and let drain. Rub with salt and pepper.
2. Melt half the butter in saucepan and lightly brown ground lamb for 3-4 minutes. Add onions and chopped poultry liver. Stir well. Add cup wine and simmer for 4-7 minutes. Add tomatoes, cinnamon, pepper, salt, and 1/2 cup water. Cover and simmer for approximately 15 minutes. Remove from heat and add pine nuts, parsley, and breadcrumbs. Stir until thoroughly combined and set aside to cool slightly.
3. Place stuffing in poultry cavity and stitch with kitchen string. Place bird in large pot with remaining butter; lightly brown on all sides. Turn breast-side up, add 1/2 cup wine. Next add 3 cups chicken broth and 3 cups water. Cover and simmer for 1 hour and 45 minutes.
4. Let bird cool slightly before removing to serving dish. Cut stitches so stuffing "tumbles out" as garnish.

Soups

BEEF AND VEGETABLE SOUP
(Soupa me lahanika ke kreas)

Ingredients

Yield: 8 servings

1 kilo beef, cut into portions
2 medium potatoes, cubed
2 medium onions, finely chopped
1 bunch celery leaves,
*   coarsely chopped*
1 bunch parsley, finely chopped
1/2 small cabbage, coarsely chopped
1/2 cup olive oil
juice of one large lemon
salt
black pepper
red pepper

Preparation

1. Rinse meat and boil in 1 1/2 liters water for 10 minutes. Strain and return to pot. Boil in one liter of fresh water for about one hour.
2. Add vegetables; cover and boil for 20 minutes.
3. Add olive oil, salt, pepper, and lemon. Boil for 8 minutes more. Serve soup hot with plenty of red pepper.

EGG-LEMON CHICKEN SOUP
(Kotosoupa avgolemono)

Ingredients

Yield: 8 servings

1 chicken
1 cup rice
3 eggs
1 lemon
salt
pepper

▲ *Soup with beef and vegetables*

Preparation

1. Place chicken in pot and cover with cold water. Bring to boil. Using slotted spoon, skim foam from surface.

2. Season with salt and pepper; cover and let simmer over low heat for about one hour.

3. Remove chicken from pot. Strain broth into a clean saucepan. Cut chicken into cubes and add to strained broth.

4. In a large, clean bowl, beat eggs with fork or wire whisk; add lemon juice and beat vigorously. Whisk in a couple of tablespoons of hot broth to heat eggs and prevent curdling when added to pot. Serve hot with plenty of freshly ground pepper.

SOUP WITH MEAT DUMPLINGS
(Soupa youvarlakia)

Ingredients

Yield: 6 servings

1/2 kilo ground beef
1 cup rice
2 Tbs. parsley, finely chopped
2 eggs
1 tsp. cumin
1/2 tsp. pepper
1 tsp. salt
2 Tbs. olive oil
juice of one large lemon

Preparation

1. Empty ground beef in mixing bowl. Make small well in middle; place egg, olive oil, salt, pepper, cumin, parsley, and rice in well. Knead by hand until thoroughly combined.

2. In large pot, bring 1 1/2 liters water to fast boil. Shape meat into round dumplings and drop into boiling water. Cook for 20 minutes. Lower heat and prepare egg-lemon sauce. (In mixing bowl, whisk egg until foamy. Gradually beat in lemon juice, alternating with a few spoonfuls of hot broth from dumplings.) Remove dumplings from heat. Let rest for 8 minutes, then add egg-lemon sauce, stir, and serve immediately. Sprinkle with pepper or parsley.

▲ *Soup with meat dumplings*

FISH

FISH STEW
(Kakkavia)

Ingredients

Yield: 8 servings

1 1/2 cups virgin olive oil
1 kilo small rock-perches
1/2 kilo blackfish or grouper
3 large potatoes, quartered
2 large onions, quartered
juice of one large lemon
salt
pepper

Preparation

1. In large pot with non-stick bottom, layer onions, potatoes, and fish. Season with salt and add water to bring level about 1 1/2 inches from top layer of fish. Pour olive oil over fish.
2. Cover pot and boil over high heat for 20 minutes. Remove lid and boil for 15 minutes more at same temperature. Remove pot from stove; add lemon juice, cover, and let stand for 10 minutes. Serve hot with lots of ground pepper.

FISH CHOWDER WITH VEGETABLES
(Psarosoupa me lahanika)

Ingredients

Yield: 8 servings

1 whole fish, about 1 kilo in weight (cod, blackfish, grouper, rock-perch)
2 medium tomatoes, quartered
1/2 kilo large zucchini (courgettes)
1/2 kilo carrots, sliced
1/2 cup olive oil
1 bunch parsley, finely chopped
1 bunch celery leaves, finely chopped
2 large potatoes, cut into chunks
2 large onions, coarsely chopped
1/2 cup rice
juice of 2 lemons
salt
freshly ground pepper

Preparation

1. Half fill large pot with water. Add one wineglass of olive oil, a pinch of salt, celery, parsley, carrots, onions, tomatoes. Boil for 20 minutes.
2. Pierce zucchini and add to pot with potatoes. Add fish; if large, cut into two or three pieces.
3. Boil ingredients together for approximately 30 minutes. With slotted spoon, remove fish and vegetables, and arrange on serving platter.
4. Select a few pieces of carrots, zucchini, and potato. Place in

blender or vegetable mill. Return puree to pot and stir into broth.

5. Bring broth to boil. Add rice. If necessary, add a little water. Boil for 20 minutes. Before removing from heat, add lemon juice.

BOURGETO
(Psarosoupa bourgeto)

Ingredients

Yield: 8 servings
1 1/2 kilos assorted rock fish plus cod, shrimp, gray mullet
700 grams onions, coarsely chopped
1 large potato, sliced
1 wine glass olive oil
1 wine glass white wine
1 wine glass water
salt
black pepper
red pepper (hot)

Preparation

Line bottom of large stew pot with onions and potato. Layer fish on top. Season fish with salt and pepper; pour oil, wine, and water over fish. Over very low heat, gradually bring to boil.
Cook on low heat, adding water if necessary, until fish is cooked and vegetables are tender.
Remove fish and place on serving platter. Serve soup with vegetables separately, then season with red pepper.

BREAM WITH CELERY
(Tsipoures me selino)

Ingredients

Yield: 6 servings
4 bream, approximately 1 1/2 kilo in total weight
1 1/2 kilo young celery hearts
1 large onion, finely chopped
1 1/2 cups olive oil
salt
pepper
2 eggs
juice of 4 lemons

Preparation

1. Clean fish, rinse, salt and let stand for 15 minutes. Heat 1/2 cup olive oil in frying pan and cook fish. Remove fish from pan and set aside. Do not discard frying oil.

2. Wash and trim celery. Cut into small pieces and blanch in boiling water. Strain. Add remaining one cup olive oil to pot and brown onions. Add celery and stir. Season with salt and pepper. Carefully arrange fish over celery. Pour frying oil and 1 1/2 cups water over fish. Bring pot to boil; cook until fish and vegetables sweat their juices.

3. When done, in separate bowl whisk eggs until foamy. Add lemon and beat well. Slowly beat in small amounts of hot broth from the pot to warm eggs so they won't curdle when added to pan. Pour egg-lemon sauce into saucepan and shake well to distribute evenly.

Remove from heat and let stand uncovered for a few minutes before serving.

OCTOPUS IN WINE
(Htapodi krassato)

Ingredients

Yield: 6 servings

1 fresh octopus, approximately 1 kilo in weight
1 1/2 cups red wine
1/2 cup olive oil
freshly ground pepper

Preparation
1. Wash octopus and clean, removing sand and ink sac as well as any ink. Cut into small pieces and rinse under cool, running water. If the octopus is very fresh, before cutting, tenderize by slapping repeatedly on hard surface or place in freezer for 24 hours.
2. Without straining, place in deep non-stick frying pan and let cook in its juices for approximately 30 minutes. Do not add water.
3. When octopus has absorbed all its liquid, add wine and olive oil. Cover and simmer for 25-30 minutes until octopus is tender and sauce has thickened.
4. Serve hot or warm in its sauce, with plenty of freshly ground pepper for guests to add according to taste.

▲ *Octopus in wine*

OCTOPUS WITH MACARONI
(Htapodi me makaronaki)

Ingredients

Yield: 8 servings

1 kilo octopus
1/2 kilo short tube pasta
2 onions, finely chopped
3-4 tomatoes, pressed through grater
200 grams olive oil
salt
pepper
cumin

Preparation
1. Clean octopus and cut into small pieces.
2. Sauté onion in olive oil until translucent. Add octopus, tomatoes, salt, pepper, cumin, and two cups water.
3. Bring to boil and cook until octopus almost tender. Add macaroni and cook for 10-15 minutes more. Serve hot.

BOILED OCTOPUS
(Htapodi vrasto me ladorigani)

Ingredients

Yield: 10 servings

1 kilo octopus, cut into medium-sized pieces
1/2 cup white wine
1/2 cup olive oil
2 Tbs. vinegar
1 tsp. oregano
1/2 tsp. salt
pinch of white pepper

Preparation
1. Boil octopus for one hour in lots of salted water. Drain. Pour wine over octopus then let drain well.
2. Arrange octopus on serving platter. Dress with olive oil and vinegar, then sprinkle with oregano and pepper. Let marinade for 3-4 hours. Serve cold.

PAN SHRIMP
(Garides saganaki)

Ingredients

Yield: 8 servings

1 kilo large shrimp
2 medium tomatoes, crushed
1 tsp. tomato paste
1 onion, finely chopped
250 grams feta cheese, hard or semi-hard
1/2 bunch parsley, finely chopped
1 chili pepper, minced
3/4 cup olive oil

▲ *Boiled octopus*

1/2 tsp. sugar (optional)
salt
freshly ground pepper

Preparation

1. Wash shrimp thoroughly. Boil in covered pot for 7-8 minutes in a small quantity of lightly salted water (about 1 1/2 cups). Strain, reserving one cup of liquid. Shell shrimp and remove heads.
2. In heavy-bottomed pan, lightly sauté onions in olive oil for 3-4 minutes. Add tomatoes, tomato paste diluted in a little water, chili pepper, salt, pepper, and sugar.
3. Simmer uncovered for 10-15 minutes, or until liquid has evaporated.
4. Add parsley, crumbled feta, and shrimp.
5. Place in ceramic serving dishes and bake in pre-heated oven at 200°C for 7-8 minutes. Serve immediately.

▲ *Pan shrimp*

FRIED CALAMARI
(Kalamarakia tiganita)

Ingredients
Yield: 8-10 servings
1 kilo calamari, sliced
1 cup olive oil for frying
salt
pepper
minced parsley
onion slices
lemon quarters

Preparation
Wash and salt calamari. Let drain liquids. Fry in olive oil until golden brown. Serve with minced parsley, lemon quarters and onions.

CALAMARI WITH TOMATO
(Kalamaria me tomata)

Ingredients
(Yield: 8 servings)
1 kilo fresh calamari (baby squid)
1 cup olive oil
1 medium onion, finely chopped
1 clove garlic, minced (optional)
1 large ripe tomato, cubed
3-4 sprigs parsley, finely chopped
salt
pepper
oregano

Preparation
1. Heat olive oil and brown onion and garlic for 3-4 minutes.
2. Clean calamari and cut into pieces. Add to onion, along with tomato, salt, pepper, oregano, and parsley.
3. Cover and let boil for 50-55 minutes. Check occasionally to make sure calamari has not boiled dry; if necessary add a little water. Remove from heat when cooked and sauce is thick.

STUFFED CALAMARI
(Kalamarakia nistissima yemista)

Ingredients
(Yield: 6 servings)
1 1/2 cups olive oil
1 kilo medium-sized calamari (baby squid)
1 large onion, finely chopped
2 spring onions, finely chopped
2 Tbs. fresh dill
3/4 cups dry white wine
2 cups rice
2 Tbs. small raisins
1/2 tsp. nutmeg
1/2 tsp. fresh ground pepper
juice of one small lemon
salt

Preparation
1. Wash and clean calamari, removing internal breast shell, and eggs. Set whole squid aside. Remove eggs and discard. Cut off heads and mince with tentacles.
2. In saucepan, heat 3 tablespoons olive oil and sauté onions for 3-4 minutes. Add minced squid parts and sauté for 3-4 minutes.

Add wine, stir, then add raisins, dill, nutmeg, dash of salt, and pepper. Cover and simmer for 10 minutes.

3. Stuff whole, cleaned calamari with mixture. Leave about 1/4 cavity unfilled, as stuffing will expand when cooked. Fasten calamari ends together with toothpick. Place calamari side-by-side in ovenproof dish. Pour olive oil, lemon juice, and half cup water over stuffed calamari. Cover with aluminum foil and bake in preheated oven at 200°C for 40-45 minutes.

4. Serve hot or at room temperature in their sauce.

▲ *Stuffed calamari*

FRIED SALTED COD
(Bakaliaros pastos tiganitos)

Ingredients

Yield: 6 servings

1 kilo salted cod
3 cups olive oil for frying
1 tsp. baking powder
1 cup flour

Preparation
1. Cut cod into pieces and soak in water for 10-12 hours. Change water at least 5-6 times during this period.
2. Rinse cod and remove large bones. Combine flour and baking powder with enough water to make a thick batter. Dip cod pieces in batter, coat, and fry.

FRESH COD WITH CELERY
(Bakaliaros freskos me selino)

Ingredients

Yield: 6 servings

1 kilo fresh cod
1 1/2 cups olive oil
2 ripe tomatoes, finely chopped
1 kilo celery (preferably celery root), chopped into medium-sized pieces
2 large onions, grated
salt
pepper

Preparation
1. Clean and bone cod. Cut into medium-sized pieces.
2. Wash and trim celery, then boil for a few minutes and drain. Brown in olive oil with onions, cooking for 7-9 minutes.
3. In clean pot, layer vegetables and fish.
4. Add tomato, a little more olive oil, salt, pepper, and one cup water. Cover and cook over medium heat for 50-55 minutes. Serve hot.

COD "BRANTADA"
(Brantada bakaliarou)

Ingredients

Yield: 6 servings

1 large boiled potato
3 cloves garlic
2 cups olive oil
5 cups strong vinegar
1 piece salted cod
2 Tbs. tomato paste
salt
1/2 tsp. sugar

Preparation
1. Cut cod into small pieces and let soak overnight in plenty of cool water. Change water 2-3 times during this period.
2. Coarsely chop potato and place in blender with garlic, 3/4 cup olive oil, and vinegar. Blend into slightly runny cream.
3. Drain cod and place on paper towels. Pat dry.
4. Heat olive oil in non-stick frying pan. Fry cod over high heat until brown on both sides. Remove

from pan. Drain on paper
towels.

5. In a clean, deep frying pan, heat 3
   tablespoons olive oil. Add tomato
   paste and 3/4 cup water, salt, and
   sugar.

6. Bring sauce to boil and cook for
   approximately 8 minutes.
   With wooden spoon, gradually stir
   in creamed garlic until
   thoroughly combined with tomato
   sauce.

7. Place cod in shallow, oven-proof
   dish. Cover with tomato-garlic
   sauce.

8. Place in slow oven for 10 minutes.
   Serve hot.

BARBECUED SARDINES
**(Sardeles yemistes
sta karvouna)**

Ingredients
                        (Yield: 8 servings)
12 large sardines
6-7 spring onions, minced
2 cloves garlic, crushed
1 Tbs. olive oil
1 tsp. ground cumin
1 bunch parsley, minced
1 egg, lightly beaten
juice of one medium lemon
salt
pepper
12 toothpicks

Preparation
1. With sharp knife, slit open
   sardine bellies and clean insides.

Gently push backbone away from
flesh and remove, snapping off at
base of head so fish head will
remain intact.

2. Rinse sardines, salt and set aside to
   drain.

3. In a small, non-stick frying pan
   lightly sauté onions with garlic for
   2-3 minutes. Add parsley,
   cumin, pepper, and lemon.
   Let cool, then add egg and
   combine with other ingredients in
   pan.

4. Stuff sardine bellies with a little
   egg-onion mix; fasten sardine
   sides with toothpick. Place
   sardines on barbecue and cook on
   each side for 3-4 minutes. Serve
   immediately with a green salad on
   the side.

BAKED SARDINES
(Sardelles sto fourno)

Ingredients

(Yield: 8 servings)

1 kilo sardines
2 cloves garlic, minced
1 large tomato, sliced
1 Tbs. parsley, minced
1/2 cup olive oil

salt – pepper

Preparation

1. Clean sardines and place in baking pan. Sprinkle with garlic and parsley; cover with tomato slices. Season with salt and pepper, then pour over olive oil.
2. Bake at 180°C for 45-50 minutes. Serve hot.

▲ *Baked sardines*

SWORDFISH KEBOBS
(Ksifias souvlaki sti schara)

Ingredients
Yield: 8 servings

1 kilo swordfish
2 green bell peppers
1 tomato
4 Tbs. flour
1 tsp. powdered mustard
3-4 Tbs. olive oil
1 lemon
1 Tbs. parsley, finely chopped
salt
pepper

Preparation
1. Rinse fish and cut into cubes. Place in a deep mixing bowl.
2. In blender, combine peppers, tomato, flour, mustard, olive oil, salt, lemon plus juice of one-half lemon into a thick sauce. Pour sauce over fish and let marinade for 2-3 hours.
3. Push swordfish onto skewers. Cook over barbecue or under oven grill for 7 minutes on each side. Sprinkle with minced parsley and serve hot with vegetable sauce on the side.

FISH WITH ROSEMARY SAUCE (SAVORO)
(Psari me saltsa dendrolivano "savoro")

Ingredients
Yield: 8 servings

1 kilo sardines or mackerel
1 1/2 cups olive oil
1 cup flour
1/2 cup red wine vinegar
salt
1 tsp. rosemary

Preparation
1. Clean fish, rinse under cool running water, and let drain. Salt and dredge with flour.
2. Heat 1 cup olive oil in frying pan; cook fish. Remove to serving platter and keep warm.
3. In clean saucepan, heat 1/2 cup olive oil. Add 1 tablespoon flour and stir vigorously with a wooden spoon. Add wine and rosemary, then simmer for 2-3 minutes. Pour over fried fish and serve immediately.

BAKED FISH WITH GREENS
(Psaria me horta ston fourno)

Ingredients
Yield: 8 servings

1 1/2 kilos fish (trout, bream, salt cod)
1 kilo spinach, finely chopped
1 bunch dill, finely chopped

Fish with rosemary sauce ▶

4-5 spring onions, finely chopped
3 cloves garlic, minced
1 Tbs. minced parsley
3/4 cup olive oil
juice of one large lemon
1 scant tsp. grated lemon rind
salt
black pepper
red pepper

Preparation
1. Clean and salt fish. Combine greens in large boil. Salt and rub together to remove water.
2. Spread greens in baking dish. Layer fish over greens. Pour olive oil and lemon juice over fish. Sprinkle with red and black pepper, lemon rind.
3. Cover with aluminum foil and bake in center of oven at 180°C for 30 minutes. Remove foil and bake for 25 minutes more. Serve hot or at room temperature.

OVEN FISH AND TOMATOES
(Psari plaki)

Ingredients
                    Yield: 8 servings
1 1/2 kilos fish, whole or sliced
5 Tbs. olive oil
5 tomatoes, chopped
2 cloves garlic, crushed
2 large onions, sliced
2 Tbs. parsley
juice of 2 lemons
1/2 cup white wine (optional)
salt
pepper
cumin

Preparation
1. Clean and scale fish. Rinse under cool running water, and then place in ovenproof dish. Pour lemon juice over fish.
2. Rinse tomatoes and slice. Crush garlic. Season fish with salt and pepper. Cover with tomatoes and onions and parsley. Pour olive oil and one cup water over vegetables and sprinkle garlic around fish. Sprinkle with cumin.
3. Add wine and a little water. Bake at 180°C for approximately one hour.

OKRA WITH FISH
(Bamyes me psari)

Ingredients
                    Yield: 8 servings
1 kilo okra
1 kilo fish fillets (sea bream, grouper)
1 medium ripe tomato, finely
   chopped
1/2 Tbs. tomato paste
1 small clove garlic, minced
1 large onion, finely chopped
1 cup olive oil
2 medium lemons
pinch of cumin
salt
pepper

Preparation
1. Wash, top and tail okra; if large, cut in half. Rinse and drain. Salt and combine with juice of one lemon. Arrange in large, shallow baking pan and let stand for one hour so

they can drain their liquid. Rinse well, and transfer to large mixing bowl.

2. In mixing bowl, toss together tomato, tomato paste diluted in juice of one lemon, garlic, onion, salt, pepper, cumin, and olive oil.

3. Place fish pieces in baking dish. Arrange okra mix around fish. Add one cup water. Cover with aluminum foil. Bake in center of oven at 180°C for 1 hour. Remove foil and bake for 20 minutes more. Serve hot or at room temperature.

SQUID WITH SPINACH AND FENNEL
(Maratha ke spanaki me soupyes)

Ingredients

Yield: 6 servings

1/2 kilo spinach
1/2 kilo fennel
1 kilo squid
1 large onion, finely chopped
juice of one lemon
salt
pepper

Preparation

1. Clean squid, removing internal shell and ink sac. Cut into small pieces and sauté in olive oil with onions until golden on all sides. Add 2 cups water, lower heat, and let simmer for

approximately 45 minutes. Test with fork to check when squid is almost tender.

2. Coarsely chop greens and add to fish. Season with salt and pepper. Stir well; cover and let simmer for 20-25 minutes. Stir and correct seasoning. Serve hot or lukewarm.

FISH IN ASPIC
(Psaropichti)

Ingredients

Yield: 8-10 servings

1 kilo fish (conger, blackfish, sea bream,
  grouper)
1/2 kilo fresh cod
1 sheet gelatin
10 whole peppercorns
1 tsp. cumin
1 onion, sliced
juice of 2 medium lemons
salt

Preparation

1. Clean fish and boil in plenty of salted water together with onion and peppercorns.

2. When fish are cooked, remove with slotted spoon. De-bone and place fillets in loaf pan. Strain fish broth and reserve.

3. Transfer broth to clean saucepan. Soak gelatin in a little cold water and add to broth with cumin and lemon juice. Boil over high heat for 4-5 minutes. Pour over fish.

4. Place loaf pan in refrigerator to cool. (Dish is best prepared a day ahead). Turn out, garnish with parsley, and sliced, hardboiled eggs.

BAKED ANCHOVIES
(Gavros me tomata ston fourno)

Ingredients

Yield: 8 servings

1 kilo large, fresh anchovies
2 cloves garlic, minced
1 Tbs. parsley, minced
1 Tbs. lemon juice
1 tsp. oregano
3 large tomatoes, sliced
3/4 cup olive oil
salt
pepper

Preparation
1. Clean fish and remove heads. Let drain liquids.
2. Salt fish; pour lemon juice over fish and arrange with garlic in large baking pan.
3. Cover fish with tomato slices. Season with salt, pepper, and oregano. Pour olive oil over top.
4. Bake at 180°C for 35-40 minutes. Serve hot or at room temperature.

BAKED MACKEREL WITH RED WINE
(Kolyi ston fourno me kokkino krassi)

Ingredients

Yield: 6 servings

6 large mackerel
2 large onions, grated
2 cloves garlic, crushed
1 cup olive oil
1 1/2 cups red wine
1 tsp. freshly ground pepper
salt

Preparation
1. Clean fish; remove insides and eggs and set aside. Remove heads and discard. Drain fish on kitchen towels. With a very sharp knife, cut fish open and carefully remove backbone.
2. In small saucepan, heat olive oil and sauté onions. Using the flat side of a knife, crush unpeeled garlic cloves. Add to onions and sauté. Add 3 tablespoons water and cook for 5-8 minutes.
3. Add pepper, salt, and wine to saucepan. Place fish in baking pan. Pour sauce over fish. Bake at 180°C for 40-50 minutes. Serve hot or at room temperature.

PAN MUSSELS
(Midia plaki)

Ingredients

Yield: 8 servings

250 grams mussels
4 medium ripe tomatoes, pressed through
  sieve or grater
4 carrots, thinly sliced
1 bunch parsley, minced
1 clove garlic, crushed
1 cup olive oil

Preparation

1. Brown carrots, parsley, garlic in olive oil. Add tomatoes, stir; cover and let simmer.
2. Just before vegetables are cooked, add mussels. Continue cooking over low heat until sauce thick. Serve at room temperature.

CRAYFISH OMELET
(Karavida omelletta)

Ingredients

Yield: 6 servings

1 kilo crayfish (or scampi)
6 eggs
1 tomato, peeled and finely chopped
1 Tbs. butter
1 Tbs. milk
salt
freshly ground pepper

Preparation

1. Boil shellfish in plenty of salted water. Drain, let cool; reserve small amount of broth. Shell crayfish, and chop into small pieces.
2. In non-stick frying pan, melt butter. Sauté shellfish and tomatoes for 7-10 minutes.
3. Beat eggs with milk and 1 tablespoon of broth. Pour mixture over shrimp and stir gently until eggs are set. Serve hot.

GRILLED RED MULLET
(Barbounia sti schara)

Ingredients

Yield: 8 servings

8 red mullets
6 Tbs. olive oil
2 Tbs. parsley, minced
juice of 1 lemon
salt
pepper

Preparation

1. Scale and clean fish. Brush with 2 tablespoons olive oil and cook over barbecue or under oven grill for 4-5 minutes on each side, according to the size of the fish.
2. Meantime, prepare oil-lemon sauce by whisking remaining olive oil with lemon juice, parsley, salt, and pepper.
3. As soon as fish is cooked, remove to serving platter; pour sauce over fish and serve immediately.

FRIED MULLET
(Barbounia Tiganita)

Ingredients

Yield: 8 servings

2 cups extra virgin olive oil
1 kilo medium-sized red mullets
1 1/2 cups flour
1 level Tbs. salt
10 lemon leaves

Preparation

1. Clean mullets, salt lightly and let drain.
2. In mixing bowl, combine flour and remaining salt. One by one dip fish in flour and coat well. Meantime, in frying pan heat olive oil until almost smoky. Shake off excess flour and fry fish in oil.
3. Brown fish on one side, then turn with fork and let brown on other side. Remove and drain on paper towels.
4. Line serving platter with lemon leaves. Arrange fish over leaves and serve.

OVEN-MARINATED MULLET
(Barbounia sti ladokolla)

Ingredients

Yield: 6 servings

6 medium mullets
6 slices lemon
1 tomato, thinly sliced
1/2 tsp. thyme
1/2 tsp. oregano
6 Tbs. olive oil
salt
pepper

Preparation

1. Clean fish, drain, and season with salt and pepper; lay each piece on a separate sheet of non-stick cooking paper (unwaxed).
2. Drizzle one tablespoon olive oil over each mullet. Sprinkle fish with oregano and thyme. Arrange one lemon slice and one tomato slice over each fish, then wrap, and seal paper around it. Bake at 200°C for 45-50 minutes.

Fried mullet ▶

BAKED RED MULLET
(Barbounia sto fourno)

Ingredients

Yield: 6 servings

6 red mullets
3 Tbs. olive oil
3 Tbs. dry white wine
juice of 1 lemon
2 cloves garlic, crushed
3 medium tomatoes, thinly sliced
salt
pepper

Preparation
1. Clean fish. Let drain liquids, then place in an oven-proof baking dish.
2. Combine olive oil, lemon juice, garlic, salt, and pepper. Pour over fish. Cover with tomato slices and bake at 180°C for 20-25 minutes. During cooking, baste with juices so fish do not dry.

FISH COOKED SPETSES-STYLE
(Psaria a la spetsiota)

Ingredients

Yield: 8 servings

1 1/2 kilo sea bream or grouper (whole, or if large 5-6 fillets)
juice of 2 large lemons
1 cup olive oil
1 onion, sliced
4 cloves garlic, finely sliced
4 large tomatoes, pushed through grater
1/2 cup dry white wine
sprig of parsley, minced
salt
pepper

Preparation
1. Clean fish. With sharp knife, pierce skin on both sides so fish will cook through.
2. Place in baking pan. Pour over lemon juice. Season with salt and pepper. Pour 1/2 cup olive oil over fish; sprinkle with flour. Let stand for approximately 1 hour.
3. In separate pan, sauté onion and garlic in remaining olive oil. Add tomatoes, parsley, and wine; cover and let simmer.
4. When sauce is ready, pour over fish and bake at 180°C for approximately 1 hour.

HERRING RICE
(Reggopilafo)

Ingredients

Yield: 8 servings

1 herring
2 cups rice
1/2 cup olive oil
1 small onion, finely chopped
1 medium tomato, peeled and diced
freshly ground pepper

Preparation
1. Rinse herring with cold water. Soak for 3 hours in tepid water. Remove skin and bones. Cut into small pieces and set aside.

2. Lightly brown onion in olive oil for 2-3 minutes. Add herring pieces and brown. Add tomato and 2-3 tablespoons water, and simmer for 5-10 minutes. Add six cups water. Stir and bring to boil. Add rice and simmer for approximately 20 minutes. Remove from heat, cover with a cotton dishtowel, and let stand for 10 minutes so towel can absorb steam. Serve with freshly ground pepper.

▲ *Herring rice*

PIES

GROUND MEAT PIE
(Pitta me kima ke portokali)

Ingredients

Yield: 8-10 servings

1 packet puff pastry
1/2 kilo ground beef
1/2 kilo ground lamb
1/2 cup olive oil
1 large onion, chopped
1 carrot, grated
1 tsp. grated orange peel
1 cup unresinated wine
1 tsp. cumin
1/2 tsp. nutmeg
2-3 cloves
1 stick cinnamon
1/2 tsp. pepper
1 Tbs. butter (for brushing filo)

Preparation
1. Lightly brown onion in olive oil. Add meat and brown, stirring continuously for 5-8 minutes. Add wine, spices; cover and simmer for 10-12 minutes.
2. Stir in orange rind and simmer for 3-4 minutes more. Remove meat filling from heat and set aside to cool.
3. Line bottom of oven-proof dish with a sheet of puff pastry. Lightly brush surface with butter. Pour filling over filling and spread evenly in pan.
4. Layer second piece of puff pastry over filling, turning ends into dish. Brush lightly with butter. Bake at 180°C for 40-45 minutes. Serve lukewarm.

NOODLE AND LEEK PIE
(Pitta me hilopittes ke prassa)

Ingredients

Yield: 8 servings

1 kilo leeks, finely chopped
250 grams short noodles
600 grams ground beef
1 1/2 cups kefalotiri cheese, grated
3 eggs
500 grams yogurt, strained
3/4 cups olive oil
1 Tbs. butter
1 small onion
3 Tbs. milk
1 Tbs. fresh mint, minced
salt
pepper

Preparation
1. Boil noodles in salted water. Strain and layer half on bottom of narrow, lightly greased baking pan. Sprinkle with one tablespoon grated cheese.
2. Wash leeks, strain, and sauté lightly in a little olive oil. Do not brown. Add one cup water, season

with salt and pepper; cover, then simmer over low heat for 20 minutes. Strain and layer over noodles.

3. Beat mint, a dash of pepper, and one egg into yogurt. Spread mixture evenly over leeks.

4. Brown meat and onion in a little olive oil. Add a little water and a dash of salt, then simmer for about 20 minutes. Using a slotted spoon, transfer meat from to baking dish and layer over yogurt mix. Spread remaining leeks over meat.

5. Melt butter and pour over leeks. Beat remaining eggs with milk and a dash of pepper.
Pour over pie and sprinkle with remaining grated cheese.
Bake at 180°C for about one hour. When golden brown crust has formed, remove from oven and let cool slightly before serving.

SPINACH PIE
(Spanakopitta)

Ingredients
Yield: 8-10 servings
• *For the crust:*
1 cup virgin olive oil
2 eggs
1 tsp. salt
1 1/2 cups milk
700 grams cake flour
1 egg yolk for glazing
1 cup sesame seeds for topping

• *For the filling:*
3 Tbs. virgin olive oil
1 kilo spinach, finely chopped
1 bunch dill, finely chopped
8 spring onions (only green stalk should be finely chopped)
2 Tbs. mint, finely chopped
2 cups sour mizithra
salt
pepper

Preparation

1. Place eggs, olive oil, milk, salt, and two cups flour in mixing bowl; using electric mixer, blend at medium speed. Gradually add flour until dough no longer sticks to the sides of the mixing bowl. Turn out on clean, lightly floured surface and knead for 4-5 minutes. Cover with cotton towel and let rest while preparing pie filling.

2. Place finely chopped spinach and dill in large bowl. Rub with salt until all greens are limp and deep green in color. Mix in spring onions, mint, pepper, and mizithra.

3. Divide dough in two. On lightly floured surface, roll out each half so that it is large enough to cover the bottom of a round baking pan. Lightly oil pan. Line with dough, letting a little hang over the sides. Pour filling over pastry and spread with back of a spoon. Cover filling with second piece of rolled out dough; seal pie by pinching the two pieces of dough together around the sides.

4. Beat egg yolk and spread over pie. Sprinkle top with sesame seeds. Bake for 40-45 minutes at 180°C. Let cool, then slice. Pie is also delicious eaten cold.

ZAGORI LEEK PIE
(*Prassopitta Zagoriou*)

Ingredients

Yield: 8 servings

• *For the crust:*
1 kilo flour
1 cup olive oil
1/2 cup olive oil for brushing dough
1 tsp. fresh yeast
1 tsp. salt
warm water

▲ *Zagori leek pie*

• *For the filling:*
1 1/2 kilo leeks
350 grams hard feta cheese
3 eggs
1/2 cup olive oil
salt
pepper
dash of cumin

Preparation

1. First make crust. Dilute yeast in 1 cup warm water, then combine in large bowl with olive oil, salt, and flour. Knead, adding enough warm to make dough smooth and elastic.
2. Cover with cotton towel and let stand for about 20 minutes, or until almost double.
3. Prepare filling by chopping leeks finely and placing in large mixing bowl. Rub leeks with salt until leeks become a deep green pulp. Place in sieve and let drain. Transfer leeks to a clean bowl and combine with feta, beaten eggs, olive oil, and pepper.
4. If using a rectangular baking pan, roll out seven sheets of filo, each roughly 50x28 cms; if using a round baking pan, sheets must be at least 60-70 cm in diameter. Filo sheets should be large enough so that a little dough hangs over the edge of the pan.
5. Generously oil pan, and lay down a sheet of filo. Brush with oil, then lay down two more sheets, brushing each with more oil. Spread 1/3 of the filling in pan, cover with a sheet of filo. Repeat with remainder of filling, then cover pie with extra sheet of filo.
6. Fold filo back over pan, making sure dough is not too thick. With sharp knife, mark slices on surface, without piercing phyllo down to the filling. Brush surface with olive oil, and bake in pre-heated oven at 170°C for about one hour until golden brown. Let cool slightly, then cut and serve. Pie is also delicious when cold.

SQUASH PIE
(Kolokithopitta)

Ingredients
Yield: 8 servings
1 kilo zucchini or squash, grated
2 large potatoes, grated
1 large onion, grated
1 cup feta cheese
1 Tbs. grated kasseri cheese
2 eggs, beaten
2 Tbs. parsley, minced
1 tsp. mint, minced
2-3 Tbs. olive oil
salt
1 tsp. freshly ground pepper
1 packet country-style filo

Preparation
1. Place squash, potatoes, and onion in colander or sieve. Salt, toss together and let stand for at least 30 minutes to drain liquids.
2. Take a fistful of grated vegetables, squeeze out water and place in a deep mixing bowl. Repeat with remaining vegetables. Combine

squash mix with cheeses, parsley, mint, salt, pepper, and eggs.

3. Lightly grease baking dish with olive oil. Arrange five sheets of filo on bottom, brushing lightly with olive oil between each sheet. Spread squash and cheese mix over filo. Arrange six sheets of filo over filling, brushing lightly with olive oil between each sheet. Using a sharp knife, trim excess filo and turn ends into pan. Mark top layer in squares, taking care not to pierce filo down to filling. Drizzle olive oil over top of pie. Bake at 190°C for 45-50 minutes.

4. Serve warm, at room temperature, or cold.

PIE WITH GRAPEVINE LEAVES, YOGURT AND HERBS
(Pitta me ambelofila, yiaourti ke aromatika horta)

Ingredients

Yield: 6 servings

3/4 kilo thick yogurt
2/3 cups corn meal
1 Tbs. fresh dill, finely chopped
1 Tbs. fresh mint, finely chopped
5-6 soft green peppercorns, minced
2 spring onions, finely chopped
salt
30-35 fresh vine leaves
1/2 cup olive oil

Preparation

1. Heat oven to 180°C. In mixing bowl, combine yogurt, corn meal, spring onions, dill, mint, and pepper, salt. Stir well.

2. Grease 22x23 cm oven-proof dish with olive oil. Use half the grape leaves to line bottom and sides.

3. Generously brush grape leaves with olive oil. Empty yogurt mix into baking dish. Cover with remaining vine leaves; brush generously with olive oil. Cover with aluminum foil and bake in medium oven at 150-180°C for 40-45 minutes.

4. Pierce pie center with sharp knife. If knife comes out clean, pie is ready. Remove from oven, let cool 15 minutes, then cut. The piece can also be served at room temperature.

NO-FILO CHEESE PIE
(Tiropitta horis filo)

Ingredients

Yield: 8-10 servings

400 grams hard feta cheese, cubed
150 grams gruyere cheese, grated
3 eggs
1 cup thick yogurt
250 grams butter
1 cup all-purpose flour
1/2 tsp. baking soda
1/2 tsp. black pepper

Preparation

1. In large mixing bowl, combine melted butter, lightly beaten eggs, baking soda, cheese, pepper, and flour. Stir until thoroughly blended.

2. Lightly butter a wide baking pan or oven-proof dish. Transfer

mixture to pan. Bake at 180°C for 30-35 minutes. Let cool slightly before cutting in small squares.

3. Serve hot or cold.

EPIRUS CHEESE PIE
(Ipirotiki tiropitta)

Ingredients

Yield: 8 servings

1/2 kilo self-raising flour
5 cups water
3 Tbs. olive oil
1/2 tsp. salt
1 Tbs. sesame seeds

• *For the filling:*
3 cups hard feta cheese, crumbled
2 eggs
1/2 tsp. black pepper

Preparation

1. In mixing bowl, combine flour, salt, water, and two tablespoons olive oil.
2. Spread half of this batter on bottom of lightly oiled baking pan (about 23 cm diameter).
3. Combine feta, eggs, and pepper. Carcfully spread over batter.
4. Pour remaining batter over filling. Sprinkle with sesame and drizzle with olive oil. Bake in preheated oven at 180°C for 75-80 minutes.
5. Let cool almost completely before cutting.

EPIRUS NEW YEAR'S PIE
(Ipirotiki Vassilopitta)

Ingredients

Yield: 8-10 servings

1 kilo lean pork from shoulder-blade, cubed
1/2 kilo chicken
3 large onions, finely chopped
1 large onion, whole
2 cups sweet trahanas
1 1/2 cups feta cheese, rubbed through grater
3-4 cloves
2 pieces celery
2 bay leaves
6 Tbs. butter
1 tsp. salt
1 tsp. pepper
1 kilo country-style filo

Preparation

1. Place two liters of water in large pot and bring to boil. Push cloves into whole onion and toss into boiling water along with bay leaves, celery, chicken, and pork. As foam rises to surface, remove with slotted spoon. Cover and boil gently for 35-40 minutes. Remove pork with slotted spoon; transfer to clean bowl to cool and drain liquids.
2. Bone chicken and finely chop meat. Heat butter in pan, then cook onions until translucent. Add chicken and pork; cook for 4-5 minutes. Add trahanas, salt, pepper, half a cup of water and cook for about 8-10 minutes more.

3. Grease bottom and sides of baking pan with butter. Line pan with one sheet of filo, then lightly butter its surface. Repeat until the bottom of the pan is lined with 3-4 sheets of filo.
Add meat mix from pan, then sprinkle feta cheese over meat. Cover filling with a sheet of filo, then lightly brush with butter; repeat with two more sheets.

With sharp knife, divide pie into squares, piercing only the top two sheets of filo. Brush surface with melted water. Dip one and in cold water, then shake wet hand over the pie so that a few drops fall lightly on surface of buttered filo. Place pie on middle rack of oven and bake at 180°C for 40-45 minutes. Remove and let cool slightly; slice and serve.

▲ *Epirus New Year's pie*

SPICY OPEN-FACED ONION PIE
(Kremmidopitta kseskepasti)

Ingredients

Yield: 8 servings

4 sheets filo
1/2 cup olive oil
800 grams onions, sliced
300 grams feta cheese, crumbled
5 eggs
1 bunch dill, finely chopped
2 Tbs. butter, melted
salt
pepper

Preparation
1. Boil onions in a little water for about 20 minutes. Strain and set aside to cool. Squeeze out excess water.
2. Beat eggs, then stir in onions, butter, feta, dill, salt, and pepper.
3. Lightly butter a round baking pan and line bottom with filo, brushing each sheet with olive oil. Let ends hang over edge of pan.
4. Spread onion and egg filling over filo. Turn filo ends towards center of pan, leaving most of the filling exposed. Brush pastry sheets with olive oil, then bake at 200°C for about 40-45 minutes.

RICE PIE
(Rizopitta)

Ingredients

Yield: 8 servings

8 sheets filo
1 1/2 cups rice
2 leeks, sliced
4 medium carrots, thinly sliced
2 onions, finely chopped
1 cup grated kefalograviera or kefalotiri cheese
5 eggs, lightly beaten
2 Tbs. butter
1/2 cup olive oil for brushing filo
3 Tbs. olive oil for filling
salt
pepper
minced parsley

Preparation
1. Sauté leeks and onions in 3 tablespoons olive oil. Add carrots and simmer for about 5 minutes.
2. Add one cup water; bring to boil. Stir in rice, then simmer for about 10 minutes. Season with salt and pepper.
3. Remove from heat; stir in eggs, cheese, parsley, and butter.
4. Lightly butter baking pan and line with 5 sheets of filo, brushing each sheet with olive oil. Let filo hang over edge of pan. Spread rice mixture over filo; turn filo ends in towards center.
5. Layer remaining filo over filling, again brushing between each sheet with olive oil. Trim ends and fold filo into pan. Brush

top of pie with olive oil, then bake at 180°C for 45-50 minutes.

POTATO PIE
(Patatopitta)

Ingredients

Yield: 8 servings

2 1/2 kilos small potatoes
1 1/2 cup grated kefalotiri
4 eggs, lightly beaten
1/2 cup dry breadcrumbs
2 medium onions, finely chopped
1/2 cup milk
1 bunch parsley, minced
butter for frying pan
olive oil for cooking

salt
pepper
oregano

Preparation
1. Scrub potatoes and boil in their skins. When cool, drain, peel, and mash.
2. Lightly sauté onion in butter, then add to pureed potatoes. Add remaining ingredients and combine thoroughly. If mixture is too runny, stir in some breadcrumbs.
3. Lightly oil baking pan. Spread puree evenly in pan.
4. With the tip of a sharp knife, mark surface into squares. Drizzle olive oil over top and bake at 200°C for about one hour, or until golden brown.

SWEETS

BAKED HALVAH
(Halvas fournou)

Ingredients

Yield: 8 servings

2 cups fine semolina
1 cup sugar
3/4 cups butter
1 cup almonds, coarsely ground
4 eggs
1 tsp. ground cinnamon

• *For the syrup:*
2 cups sugar
3 cups water
1 tsp. grated lemon peel

Preparation
1. Using electric mixer, cream butter and sugar until pale and fluffy.
2. On medium speed, beat in eggs one at a time.

▲ Halvah

Add semolina, then almonds.

3. Lightly butter baking pan. Pour semolina mixture into pan; spread evenly with spatula so that mixture is not over 3 cm thick.

4. Bake in medium oven for about 40 minutes. Meantime, prepare syrup: bring water, sugar, lemon peel, and one stick cinnamon to boil, stirring continuously. Remove from heat and let cool completely.

5. Remove halvah from oven and immediately pour cool syrup over pan.

SEMOLINA HALVAH
(Halvas)

Ingredients
                        Yield: 10 servings
1 1/2 cups virgin olive oil
1 package fine wheat semolina
1 cup flour
ground cinnamon

• *For the syrup:*
3 cups sugar
1 tsp. grated lemon peel

Preparation
1. In heavy-bottomed saucepan, heat olive oil until smoky. Add semolina and stir quickly with wooden spoon until semolina starts to brown. Add flour and stir vigorously.

2. Meantime, have syrup prepared and ready. (Thoroughly dissolve sugar in eight cups boiling water).

3. Continue stirring semolina mix over heat until dark brown, then slowly add syrup. Stir continuously, taking care not to let semolina and syrup boil over. When the semolina has absorbed all the syrup, remove from heat, stir in cinnamon, cover with a cotton dishtowel. Let stand for approximately 10 minutes.

4. Spoon halvah onto a serving platter, preferably lined with leaves from a lemon tree or bitter orange tree. Dust with cinnamon and serve.

COPENHAGEN
(Kopenhayi)

Ingredients
                        Yield: 10-12 servings
1 packet ready filo
2 cups sugar
2 1/2 cups almonds, finely chopped
1 cup fine wheat semolina or dry breadcrumbs
2 eggs
1 tsp. baking powder
1 tsp. cinnamon
1/2 tsp. salt
1 cup butter

• *For the syrup:*
3 cups sugar

2 cups water
1 tsp. glucose

Preparation
1. Place sugar in a stainless steel or enamel mixing bowl. Break eggs into sugar and whisk until thick.
2. Add almonds, semolina, baking powder, cinnamon and salt. With a wooden spoon, stir until mixture is thoroughly blended and forms a thick paste.
3. Butter bottom and sides of a rectangular baking dish about 5-6 cm deep. Line with filo, lightly buttering between each sheet. Let filo hang over pan's rim. Spread almond mix evenly over filo. Turn filo ends in towards center.
4. Cover with remaining filo, brushing with butter between each sheet. Trim excess filo. Mark top sheet in diamond-shaped pieces but do not pierce down to filling. Pour remaining butter over top and bake in preheated oven at 180°C for 50-55 minutes.
5. Prepare syrup and let cool completely. Remove «Copenhagen» from oven and immediately pour syrup over pan. Cool completely before serving.

IOANNINA «KADAIFI»
(Kadaifi yianiotiko)

Ingredients
Yield: 10-12 servings
1 package ready-made filo
1 package kadaifi pastry
1 1/2 cups butter
2 cups almonds
1 cup dry breadcrumbs
1 Tbs. ground cinnamon

• *For the syrup:*
5 cups sugar
1 Tbs. glucose
4 cups water

Preparation
1. Coarsely chop almonds. Mix well with cinnamon and breadcrumbs.
2. On a flat surface, cut filo into 5-7 cm strips. Take one strip, brush with butter, and place another strip on top. Sprinkle with kadaifi along length of filo strip. Spoon some almond mix near the edge, and roll tightly. Place roll in buttered baking dish. Repeat until all filling has been used.
3. Mark each strip into pieces. Pour remaining butter over top and sprinkle with water.
4. Bake at 180°C for approximately 40 minutes. Remove from oven and let cool completely. Prepare syrup and pour hot over pan.

YOGURT WITH PRESERVES OR HONEY
(Yiaourti me gliko koutaliou i meli)

Ingredients
Yield: 4 servings

1/2 kilo thick, strained yogurt
4 tsp. rose or fig preserves or 4 tsp.
   honey
1 Tbs. coarse walnut pieces

Preparation
   Spoon yogurt into four serving
bowls. Garnish with preserves. If
using honey, sprinkle with
walnuts.

RAVANI WITH YOGURT
(Yiaourtoravani)

Ingredients
Yield: 12 servings

6 eggs
800 grams full-fat yogurt
300 grams sugar
1 Tbs. butter, melted
600 grams white cake flour
1 tsp. baking powder

• *For the syrup:*
600 grams sugar
1/2 liter water
3-4 drops lemon juice

Preparation
1. In mixing bowl, beat yogurt
    and sugar until thick and
    creamy.
2. Add lightly beaten egg yolks and
    melted butter.

3. In separate bowl, beat egg
    whites until stiff. Gently fold in
    flour and baking powder.
    Stirring continuously, add egg
    white and flour mix to yogurt and
    sugar.
4. Turn mixture into a large, shallow,
    lightly buttered baking dish. (Batter
    should not be more than one inch
    thick).
5. Bake at 180°C for 15 minutes. Then
    turn off heat from top and bake,
    from bottom only, for 30 minutes
    more.
6. Remove from oven and let cool
    completely. Prepare syrup and pour
    hot over ravani cake.

SEMOLINA HONEY COOKIES
(Melomakarona apla me simigdali)

Ingredients
Yield: 40-50 cookies

3 1/2 cups extra virgin olive oil
1 1/2 cups powdered sugar
1 cup honey
juice of four oranges
1 tsp. baking soda
1 tsp. baker's ammonia
1/2 tsp. ground cinnamon
3-4 cloves, ground
3 cups cake flour
1 1/2 cups fine semolina
2-3 sheets waxed paper
1 Tbs. butter

Yogurt with preserves ▶

134

• *For the syrup:*
1 kilo sugar
4 cups water
2 cups walnuts, finely chopped

Preparation
1. Dilute baker's ammonia and baking soda in orange juice. In large bowl, combine juice with olive oil, powdered sugar, cinnamon, cloves, and honey. Mix by hand, until thoroughly combined.
2. Gradually add flour and semolina, alternating between the two until a soft dough forms. Shape small pieces of dough into oblong cookies; place on lightly buttered sheet of wax paper.
3. Bake at 180°C for 20-25 minutes. Meantime, prepare syrup and let cool completely. When cookies are baked, remove from oven. While cookies are still hot, immerse in cool syrup for 3-4 minutes; use a slotted spoon to dip and remove cookies from syrup. After dipping, arrange on a serving platter and sprinkle with chopped walnuts.

«KOURABIEDES»
(Kourambiedes)

Ingredients
Yield: 60-70 cookies
500 grams margarine
400 grams butter
2 cups sugar
800 grams almonds

3 egg yolks
1 egg white, beaten stiff
2 Tbs. brandy
1/2 tsp. vanilla
1 tsp. cinnamon
1 tsp. baking soda
1 Tbs. lemon juice
1 1/2 cups flour
3-4 cups powdered sugar

Preparation
1. In mixing bowl, cream butter and margarine together, then add sugar and brandy. Beat until light and creamy. Meantime, roast almonds in medium oven for 7-12 minutes. Remove and chop, either finely or coarsely according to taste.
2. To the butter mixture, gradually add egg yolks. Beat thoroughly for 2-3 minutes more.
3. Dilute baking soda in lemon juice; add to butter mix, along with cinnamon, almonds, vanilla. Gradually blend in beaten egg white. Slowly stir flour into mix, and knead into thick dough.
4. With your hands, shape pieces of dough into circles or crescent shapes, and place on lightly buttered cookie sheet. Bake at 200°C for 20-25 minutes.
5. Remove cookies from oven and let cool completely. Dredge with powdered sugar.

"Kourabiedes" ▶

BAKED QUINCE WITH HONEY AND MAVRODAFNI WINE
(Kidonia psitta me meli ke Mavrodafni)

Ingredients

Yield: 8 servings

4 quinces, with peel and cut
   in half
1 Tbs. whole cloves
2 cups Mavrodafni wine (or sherry)
1 cup red wine
3-4 Tbs. honey
1 tsp. ground cinnamon
2 cups thick yogurt

Preparation
1. Heat oven to 180°C. Core quinces, removing tough hearts. Place in oven-proof dish, cut side down. Push 2-3 cloves into skin of each quince half.
2. Heat Mavrodafni and wine. Stir in honey and cinnamon. Pour sauce over quince halves and bake for approximately 90 minutes. Baste frequently with syrup from pan.
3. Let cool. Place cut side up in serving dish. Spoon yogurt into cavity.

MERINGUE KISSES
(Bezedes)

Ingredients

Yield: 15-20 pieces

4 egg whites
1 cup powdered sugar
2 cups granulated sugar
1/2 tsp. vanilla
1 level Tbs. butter
1 Tbs. flour
Juice of half lemon

Preparation
1. Place granulated sugar in heavy-bottomed saucepan with half cup water and lemon juice. Let simmer until sugar is completely dissolved and forms a thick syrup. Remove from heat before syrup starts to turn yellow and place in lightly preheated oven to keep warm.
2. Beat egg whites until very stiff.
3. Gradually whisk syrup into egg whites until absorbed. Slowly whisk in powdered sugar and vanilla. Give mix final few turns with a wooden spoon.
4. Line cookie sheet with wax paper. Lightly butter and flour. Spoon meringue onto sheet. Shape into oblongs with a soup spoon or use pastry funnel to create fancy shapes.
5. Bake for approximately 20 minutes in medium oven. Let cool completely and remove from paper. Serve plain or make meringue «sandwiches» with strawberry, raspberry or orange marmalade.

TANGERINE FONDANT
(Fondan mandariniou)

Ingredients
Yield: 30-40 pieces
Peel of 6 large tangerines
2 cups blanched almonds
2 cups sugar
1 1/2 cups sugar for dipping

Preparation
1. Lightly roast almonds and chop coarsely. Thoroughly wash tangerine peel and boil in plenty of water until soft. Drain. Let stand for 20 minutes, then puree in vegetable mill.
2. Place tangerine puree in saucepan with sugar, almonds, and 2-3 tablespoons water. With wooden spoon, stir over low heat for 25-40 minutes, or until mixture shrinks from sides of saucepan.
3. Remove from heat and let cool completely. Take small piece of soft candy and shape into a walnut-sized ball. Roll in sugar and place in center of paper candy cup. Let stand for 4-5 hours, then refrigerate for 10 hours more until completely hard. Fondant will keep refrigerated for up to 30 days.

MILK PIE
(Galaktoboureko)

Ingredients
Yield: 8-10 servings
1/2 cup fine semolina
1 1/2 cups sugar
1/2 cups cornstarch
6 eggs, lightly beaten
1 liter milk
1/2 cup semolina
12 sheets filo
130 grams butter
1 tsp. grated lemon peel (optional)

• *For the syrup:*
1 tsp. lemon juice
1 1/2 cups sugar
3/4 cup water
1 cinnamon stick

Preparation
1. In mixing bowl, combine 1/4 cup semolina, sugar, cornstarch, eggs, grated lemon peel. Stir until thoroughly blended.
2. In saucepan, heat milk to boiling. Gradually whisk into semolina mixture.
3. Transfer milk and semolina mixture back to saucepan and heat while stirring continuously. Gradually add remaining semolina; do not bring mixture to a boil. Remove from heat and set aside semolina cream to cool.
4. Butter 22x30 cm oven-proof baking dish. Line with a sheet of filo. Let filo hang over edge of pan. Brush generously with

melted butter. Repeat five
times.

5. Pour semolina cream into pan,
spreading evenly over filo. Cover
with remaining filo sheets,
brushing each sheet with melted
butter. Trim and tuck filo edges into
baking dish.

6. Brush surface with melted butter.
With a sharp knife, mark
squares on top sheet, taking care
not to pierce down to filling. Bake
at 180°C for 45 minutes. Meantime,
prepare syrup and let cool
completely.

7. Remove milk pie from oven and
while still hot, brush surface with
melted butter, then pour cooled
syrup over pie.

HONEYED CHEESE PIE
(Mizithropita tapsiou me meli)

Ingredients

Yield: 6 servings
1 kilo fresh sweet mizithra cheese
4 tablespoons thyme honey
juice of one lemon
1 Tbs. grated lemon rind
6 eggs
1 tsp. fresh mint, finely chopped

Preparation

1. In mixing bowl, combine mizithra,
honey, lemon juice, grated lemon
peel, and eggs. Use electric mixer to
ensure all ingredients are
thoroughly combined.

2. When thoroughly mixed, stir in
chopped mint.

3. Butter an oven-proof dish. Place
mixture in dish and bake at 180°C
for 30 minutes, until puffy and
lightly browned.

4. Serve hot.

RICE PUDDING WITH EGGS AND GRATED LEMON PEEL
(Rizogalo me avga ke ksisma lemoniou)

Ingredients

Yield: 6 servings
1 liter milk
1 cup short-grain rice
6 Tbs. sugar
2 Tbs. corn starch
2 egg yolks
grated lemon peel
pinch of salt

Preparation

1. Place two cups water and
pinch of salt in small saucepan.
Add rice and boil until liquid has
been absorbed.

2. Dilute corn starch in one cup
lukewarm milk. Add to rice, stirring
continuously with a wooden spoon.
Add remaining milk.

3. Beat egg yolks with sugar until
thick. Add to milk and rice
mixture, stirring continuously
until pudding thickens. Stir in
grated lemon peel. Spoon into
individual bowl and serve.

RAISIN BREAD
(Stafidopsomo)

Ingredients

Yield: 2 loaves

1 1/2 cups lukewarm milk and water
2 Tbs. fresh yeast
3 cups all-purpose flour
2 1/2 cups whole-wheat flour
2 Tbs. sugar
pinch of salt
1 cup olive oil
1 cup whole raisins
1/2 cup walnuts, finely chopped
1/2 tsp. ground cinnamon

Preparation
1. Dilute yeast in half of the milk-water.
2. In a separate, larger mixing bowl combine the two types of flour and make a well in the middle. Pour yeast mix into the center of the well, then add remaining milk-water, sugar, cinnamon, salt and 1/2 cup olive oil.
3. Knead ingredients into slightly sticky dough. If necessary, add more flour. Cover with cotton kitchen towel for approximately two hours, or until double in size.
4. Turn dough out onto lightly floured surface. Punch down; knead in walnuts and raisins.
5. Shape dough into one large loaf or several small loaves. Place in greased pans and bake in warm oven for 30 minutes. Then bake at 180°C for one hour, or until lightly browned.

SWEET EASTER BREAD WITH GRATED ORANGE
(Tsoureki Paschalino me ksisma portakaliou)

Ingredients

Yield: 3 loaves

1 1/2 kilo flour
1 Tbs. fresh yeast
1 tsp. baking powder
1 cup orange juice
1 Tbs. grated orange peel
2 eggs
2 cups plus 2 Tbs. sugar
2 Tbs. butter
1 1/2 cups milk
3 pieces mastic, crushed
1/2 tsp. ground cinnamon
2-3 mahlepi corns, crushed
1/2 tsp. salt
1 cup olive oil

Preparation
1. In small mixing bowl, dilute yeast in 1 1/2 cups lwarm milk. Add enough flour to form a soft dough. Cover with cotton dish towel and let rise in warm place until double in size.
2. In a large mixing bowl, combine remaining flour with baking powder and make well in the center. Place risen dough, eggs, butter, orange juice, grated orange peel, sugar, salt, and flavorings into well. Knead for 10-12 minutes, continuously dipping hands in warm water and olive oil. If using electric mixer, knead dough at low speed.

3. Cover dough with two cotton dish towels. Let rise for at least one hour, until double in size.

4. Preheat oven at 200°C for 10 minutes, then turn off heat. Separate dough into three pieces, roll into strips, then braid. Place loaf (or loaves, if you wish to make smaller braids) on lightly greased cookie sheets. Place in warm oven and let rest for 10 minutes. Remove from oven, brush with beaten egg and bake at 180°C for 50-60 minutes until golden brown and hard on bottom.

CHRISTMAS BREAD WITH ALMONDS
(Christopsomo me mahlepi ke amigdala)

Ingredients

Yield: 2 loaves

5-6 cups all-purpose flour
1 cup olive oil
1 1/2 cups sugar
2 packets dry yeast
1 cup orange juice
2 cloves, ground
1/2 tsp. mahlepi, ground
1 small piece Chios mastic, crushed
2 Tbs. almonds, coarsely ground
10 whole almonds, blanched
1 unshelled walnut
pinch of salt

Preparation

1. Place half the flour in mixing bowl. Make well in center. Dissolve yeast in one cup warm water and pour into well. Slowly stir into flour to form a thick batter. Cover with a cotton dishtowel and let stand in a warm place until double in size.

2. When dough has risen, add olive oil, orange juice, sugar, spices, salt, ground almonds; slowly knead in remaining flour.

3. Using circular motions, knead dough until smooth and soft. Turn out on to lightly floured surface and knead for 4-5 minutes more.

4. Shape dough into one large or two small round loaves. Transfer to lightly oiled baking sheet. Place walnut in center of loaf. Arrange almonds in the shape of a cross, with walnut at the center.

5. Cover loaf and let stand until double. When risen, brush surface with a little olive oil or sugar water. Bake at 180°C for 55-60 minutes.

SANTORINI «MELITINIA»
(Melitinia Santorinis)

Ingredients

Yield: 30 cookies

• *For the filling:*
1 kilo unsalted anthotiro cheese
5 Tbs. sugar

4 eggs
1 Tbs. butter
2 Tbs. flour
3 pieces mastic, crushed

• *For the filo:*
1/2 kilo flour
2 Tbs. butter
1 level tsp. baking soda
pinch of salt
1 cup lukewarm water

Preparation

1. Combine anthotiro with sugar, eggs, butter, flour, and crushed mastic.
2. Prepare filo: Dilute soda in tepid water and combine with remaining ingredients. Knead into a smooth dough.
3. On floured surface, roll out dough to 1-2 mm thickness. Place saucer on dough and cut into circles 5-6 cm in diameter. Place one full tablespoon of filling near the center of each circle; fold dough over filling and pinch sides together with a fork.
4. Place «melitinia» on buttered cookie sheet. Bake in preheated oven until golden.
5. Remove from oven and dust with ground cinnamon. Let cool.

MILK PIE
(Galatopitta)

Ingredients

Yield: 8-10 servings

5 sheets filo
1 liter milk
1 cup coarse semolina
1 cup sugar
6 eggs
2 Tbs. butter
2 vials vanilla powder
1 tsp. cinnamon
2 Tbs. sugar

Preparation

1. In saucepan, heat milk to boiling. Add semolina and stir with wooden spoon. Remove from heat and let cool slightly.
2. Cream one cup sugar with 4 eggs and vanilla. Slowly stir mixture into saucepan with semolina and milk. Return to stove; stir over slow heat until mixture is thick and creamy.
3. Lightly butter bottom and sides of a round baking pan. Layer bottom with two sheets of filo, brushing each one with butter. Sprinkle with a little sugar and cinnamon, then layer with two more sheets of filo. Sprinkle with a little more sugar and cinnamon, then layer one more sheet of filo on top. Spread cream over filo; turn filo ends in towards center of pan.
4. Vigorously beat two eggs with a

little melted butter.
Pour over pie. Bake at 180°C

for 45-55 minutes.
Serve warm.

▲ *Milk pie*

NUT CRESCENTS
(Skaltsounia me ksirous karpous)

Ingredients
Yield: about 30 pieces
• *For the dough:*
3/4 cups extra virgin olive oil
2 eggs, lightly beaten
1/2 tsp. salt
1 1/2 cups water
about 700-800 grams flour
2 cups sugar
1 tsp. ground cinnamon

• *For the filling:*
2 cups coarsely ground walnuts
2 cups coarsely ground almonds
2 cups dry breadcrumbs
1 Tbs. sugar
1 tsp. cinnamon
4-5 cloves, crushed
1 Tbs. grated orange peel
3 Tbs. honey

Preparation
1. In large mixing bowl, thoroughly combine all filling ingredients.
2. In separate bowl, combine olive oil, eggs, salt, and water; gradually stir in enough flour to create a soft dough. Let rest for about 20 minutes.
3. Roll out dough and cut into small circles, about 9-10 cms in diameter. Place a spoonful of filling in circle, then fold dough over filling to create a half-moon shape. Press dough together around edges to seal.
4. Lightly oil two baking sheets. Transfer crescents to cookie sheets and bake at 180°C for 50-60 minutes.
5. Remove from oven and let cool for about 15-20 minutes. Dredge with powdered sugar and ground cinnamon.

«LOUKOUMADES»
(Loukoumades)

Ingredients
Yield: 10 servings
500 grams flour
600 grams lukewarm water
1 tsp. salt
1 pea-sized piece of mastic, crushed with one tablespoon sugar
15 grams fresh yeast

• *For the syrup:*
1 kilo sugar
1 liter water

Preparation
1. Boil water and sugar until desired thickness is achieved. Dissolve yeast in half the tepid water. Pour into mixing bowl and combine with flour, salt, and mastic to form a loose dough.
2. Stir in remaining water (which must be lukewarm so dough will rise quickly). Let dough stand in warm place. The temperature of the place where the dough is left to rise is especially important; if warm enough, dough will rise in

45-60 minutes. Dough is ready to use when bubbles have formed on surface.

3. Take fistful of dough and squeeze out dollops of dough into hot olive oil. Use spoon to separate dough balls.

4. Stir continuously while frying to cook evenly and prevent sticking. Remove with slotted spoon, quickly drain on kitchen towels; pour syrup over puffs and serve.

ALMOND BAKLAVA
(Baklavas me amigdala ke karidia)

Ingredients

Yield: 10 servings

1 packet filo
2 cups almonds and walnuts, coarsely
  chopped
3 Tbs. sugar
1 tsp. cinnamon
1 piece mastic, crushed with a little
  sugar
10-15 whole cloves
1 cup butter

• For the syrup:
2 cups sugar
1 cup water
1 cinnamon stick

▲ *"Loukoumades"*

Preparation
1. In mixing bowl, combine sugar with nuts, ground cinnamon, and mastic.
2. Lightly oil bottom and sides of shallow baking pan. Layer bottom with 5 or 6 sheets of filo, brushing with butter between each sheet. Let ends hang over edge of pan.
3. Spread nut filling evenly over filo. Layer remaining filo over top, always brushing with butter between each sheet. Trim excess filo and turn ends into pan. Drizzle a little butter over top.

With tip of sharp knife, mark baklava into diamond-shape pieces, taking care not to pierce down to the filling. Push a clove into center of each diamond.
4. Bake at 180°C for 50-55 minutes, or until filo is golden brown. Meanwhile, prepare syrup and let cool. When baklava is done, remove from oven, drizzle a little butter over top, then immediately pour cold syrup over pan. Let baklava stand for awhile to soak up syrup before cutting and serving.

▲ *Almond baklava*

SWEET CHEESE CUPS
(Glika "kalathakia" me mizithra)

Ingredients

Yield: about 30 pieces

240 grams butter
160 grams sugar
2 eggs
4 cups flour

• *For the filling:*
1 kilo soft cheese (ricotta)
1 egg
3 Tbs. sugar
1 egg yolk for glazing
ground cinnamon

Preparation

1. Using electric mixer, cream butter and sugar on medium speed for about 3-4 minutes. Add eggs and gradually beat in flour until a soft, light dough forms. Divide dough among small, lightly greased tart pans and pat down to form crust.
2. Combine filling ingredients. Spoon mixture over dough. Brush surface with beaten egg yolk, then sprinkle with cinnamon. Bake in preheated oven at 180°C for 30 minutes. Let pies cool before removing from tins. Eat cold.

"KSEROTIGANA"
(Kserotigana)

Ingredients

Yield: 8-10 servings

1 kilo hard flour
2 Tbs. raki, tsipouro, or grappa
1 Tbs. olive oil
1 tsp. salt
2-3 cups water
3-4 cups sunflower oil or corn oil

• *For the syrup:*
1 kilo sugar
1 cup honey
1/2 liter water
1 cinnamon stick
1 cup walnuts, finely ground
1 Tbs. sesame seeds

Preparation

1. Measure flour into large mixing bowl. Make slight well in center. Pour raki, olive oil, salt, and water into well. Knead on medium speed for about 10 minutes or until a smooth, slightly hard dough forms. Cover and let rest for about 10 minutes.
2. Divide dough into two pieces. Roll out each piece until about 1 cm thick. Cut into strips 2-3 cms wide and 15 cms long. Roll up each strip into a large rosebud-like shape.
3. Fry each rosebud in hot oil for 3-4 minutes, or until light golden brown.
4. Drain on kitchen paper.
5. Prepare syrup by boiling sugar,

Kserotigana, kalitsounia, and skaltsounia ▶

honey, water, and cinnamon together for 10-13 minutes. Dip each rosebud in hot syrup. Arrange on serving platter; sprinkle with ground walnuts and sesame seeds.

BAKED RICE PUDDING
(Rizogalo fournou)

Ingredients

Yield: 8 servings

1 cup rice
2 cups water
1 kilo milk
4 Tbs. corn starch
6 Tbs. sugar
grated peel of one lemon
4 eggs, beaten
1 Tbs. ground cinnamon
2 vials vanilla powder

Preparation
1. Bring water to boil; add rice. When liquid has been absorbed, add milk, reserving one-half cup.
2. Heat half cup milk. Dissolve corn starch in warmed milk.
3. Add corn starch to rice. Stir in sugar and lemon rind. Continue stirring until mixture thickens. When pudding consistency is reached, remove from heat and let cool slightly.
4. Add eggs and cinnamon, stirring vigorously to prevent eggs from setting.
5. Transfer mixture to a buttered oven-proof dish. Bake at 180°C for

about 45 minutes or until light golden brown. Serve cold.

"KALITSOUNIA"
(Kalitsounia)

Ingredients

Yield: about 40 pieces

• *For the dough:*
1 cup butter
2 egg yolks
1 Tbs. sugar
1 cup milk
5-6 cups soft flour
1 tsp. ground cinnamon

• *For the filling:*
1 kilo ricotta cheese
3 Tbs. sugar
2 eggs
1/2 tsp. grated orange peel

Preparation
1. Measure flour into mixing bowl. Make well in center. Pour melted butter into well, with egg yolks, half the milk, and sugar. Knead ingredients together, adding remaining milk as needed to form a soft, smooth dough.
2. Divide dough in three. Roll out each piece until about 1 cm thick. Cut into circles, about 4-5 cms in diameter.
3. Combine cheese, sugar, 1 egg, and grated peel.
4. Place a spoonful of filling in center of each dough circle.

Carefully push dough in from edges to form small tarts. Brush surface of each tart with beaten egg and sprinkle with cinnamon. Bake at 180°C for 25-35 minutes.

"RAVANI"
(Ravani)

Ingredients

Yield: 10 servings

500 grams fine semolina
250 grams soft flour
1/2 kilo full-fat yogurt
50 grams sugar
2 cups milk
12 eggs
1 tsp. baking powder
2 vials vanilla powder
1 tsp. butter

▲ *"Ravani"*

• *For the syrup:*
2 kilos sugar
1 liter water
2 slices lemon peel

Preparation
1. In large mixing bowl, combine semolina, flour, and baking powder.
2. Beat eggs with sugar until pale and fluffy. Whisk in milk plus one cup water. Slowly stir egg mixture into flour; add vanilla and stir until ingredients are thoroughly combined. Add yogurt and stir vigorously to create a smooth, slightly loose batter.
3. Butter a large baking pan. Pour batter into pan. Bake at 180°C for 50-60 minutes. Remove from oven and let cool.
4. Prepare syrup by bringing all ingredients to boil over low heat until thick and pale yellow.
5. Pour hot syrup over cool semolina cake. Let stand for at least one hour before serving.

RAISIN PANCAKES
(*Tiganites me stafides*)

Ingredients
                        Yield: 10-12 servings
2 cups all-purpose flour
2 Tbs. sugar
2 Tbs. raisins
2 cups water
1/2 tsp. salt
4 tsp. baking powder
olive oil or corn oil for frying
powdered sugar
ground cinnamon

Preparation
1. Sift flour with baking powder and salt. Rinse raisins and drain on kitchen paper.
2. In large mixing bowl, combine flour, raisins, sugar, and water to form a thick batter. Beat vigorously with wood spatula. Cover with plastic wrap and let rise for 30 minutes.
3. Heat frying oil. Pour batter into oil to form pancakes. When golden brown on both sides, remove with slotted spoon and arrange on serving platter.
4. Sprinkle with powdered sugar and cinnamon. Serve hot.

SAUCES

EGG LEMON SAUCE
(Saltsa avgolemono)

Ingredients
3 eggs
1 lemon
2 Tbs. broth

Preparation
Break eggs and separate whites and yolks. Beat egg whites until white and foamy (they do not need to form peaks). Beat in egg yolks one at a time. Beat in lemon juice a few drops at a time. While still beating, slowly add a small amount of warm broth from dish to which egg-lemon sauce will be added.

LEMON AND OLIVE OIL SAUCE
(Saltsa ladolemono)

Ingredients
4 Tbs. lemon juice
8 Tbs. olive oil
1 Tbs. parsley, minced
salt
pepper

Preparation
Place lemon juice in mixing bowl. Using a fork, slowly beat in olive oil a few drops at a time until sauce is thick and clear. When all the olive oil has been beaten into the lemon juice, season with salt and pepper; stir in parsley.
This sauce is used to baste meat and fish while being grilled. Remaining sauce is then served at the table to be spooned over cooked meat or fish.

BECHAMEL SAUCE
(Saltsa bechamel)

Ingredients
6 level Tbs. butter
7-8 level Tbs. flour
4 cups milk
1-2 egg yolks, beaten
salt
pepper

Preparation
Melt butter in wide saucepan over low heat. Slowly add flour, stirring continuously with a wooden spoon or whisk until all the flour has been incorporated into the butter. Meanwhile, in a separate saucepan, heat milk but do not let boil.
When butter and flour have been thoroughly combined, add hot milk while stirring continuously to prevent lumps. Cook sauce until thick and creamy. Remove from heat, season with salt and pepper; whisk in egg yolks.

MINT SAUCE
(Saltsa diosmou)

Ingredients
5-6 tender mint leaves, minced
sprig of parsley, minced
1-2 Tbs. vinegar
1 level tsp. sugar
salt
pepper

Preparation
Combine mint and parsley in a
sauceboat. Add vinegar, sugar, salt,
pepper and enough hot water so that
mint floats. Stir vigorously.

TOMATO SAUCE
(Saltsa tomata)

Ingredients
4 large ripe tomatoes
2 Tbs. olive oil
1/2 tsp. sugar
1 small onion, finely chopped
1 clove garlic, finely chopped
salt
pepper

Preparation
1. Rinse tomatoes and remove stems.
2. Place in saucepan, cover with water
   and bring to boil. When slightly
   tender, remove, drain, crush.
3. Add remaining ingredients to
   tomato pulp and bring to boil over
   low heat; cook until sauce thickens.

LEMON-OLIVE OIL DRESSING WITH PARSLEY OR DILL
(Saltsa ladolemono me maidano i anitho)

Ingredients
1 cup extra virgin olive oil
5 Tbs. lemon juice
1 scant tsp. salt
1/2 cup parsley or dill, minced
2-3 drops warm water

Preparation
Place ingredients in a deep mixing bowl
or a glass screw-top jar. Whisk or shake
until all ingredients are thoroughly
combined.

OREGANO, THYME, HONEY AND OLIVE OIL DRESSING
(Saltsa me rigani, thimari, meli ke eleolado)

Ingredients
3/4 cup olive oil
1 tsp. thyme
1 tsp. oregano
1/2 Tbs. honey
1 Tbs. lemon juice
2-3 drops warm water

Preparation
In mixing bowl, whisk olive oil with
honey, warm water, and lemon juice
until thoroughly combined. Add thyme
and oregano, and beat for 3-4 minutes
more.

BUTTERMILK AND OLIVE OIL DRESSING
(Saltsa me ksinogala ke eleolado)

Ingredients
4 Tbs. extra virgin olive oil
1 cup buttermilk
4 cloves garlic
1 Tbs. mint, minced
salt

Preparation
1. Using mortar and pestle or blender, pulverize garlic and salt.
2. Place garlic pulp in mixing bowl. Add buttermilk, olive oil, and mint; whisk or beat with fork for 2-3 minutes.
3. Cover with plastic wrap and refrigerate for 2-3 hours. Serve with fried zucchini, eggplant, or potatoes.

IONIAN AIOLI
(Eptanisiaki alioli)

Ingredients
1 cup extra virgin olive oil
5 cloves garlic
2 egg yolks
1 Tbs. white wine vinegar
1/2 tsp. salt

Preparation
1. In mortar and pestle, crush garlic with salt. Place garlic pulp in blender; add egg yolks, which have been lightly whisked with the vinegar.
2. Turn on blender. Add in oil, drop by drop, until it has been absorbed and sauce is smooth and thick.

Notes

NOTES

NOTES

NOTES